MW01226896

I Know You By Heart

A Love Story

"Our love is like a hidden treasure
That once found is prized above all else"

Joan Saner Harder

WEST BOW
P R E S S
A DIVISION OF THOMAS NELSON

WestBow Press books may be ordered through booksellers or by contacting:

WestBow Press
A Division of Thomas Nelson
1663 Liberty Drive
Bloomington, IN 47403
www.westbowpress.com
1-(866) 928-1240

Because of the dynamic nature of the Internet, any web addresses or
links contained in this book may have changed since publication and
may no longer be valid. The views expressed in this work are solely those
of the author and do not necessarily reflect the views of the publisher,
and the publisher hereby disclaims any responsibility for them.

Any people depicted in stock imagery provided by Thinkstock are models,
and such images are being used for illustrative purposes only.

Certain stock imagery © Thinkstock.

ISBN: 978-1-4497-1165-8 (sc)
ISBN: 978-1-4497-1166-5 (e)

Library of Congress Control Number: 2011921053

Printed in the United States of America

WestBow Press rev. date: 3/30/2011

Dedication

To Will,
The love of my life
Who left an amazing legacy
I dedicate these words to you and our four wonderful
children,
Mike, Lorna, Lisa, Chris and their families
to carry on where you left off.

❧

"You could never be gone, because you live inside of me
for ever and ever.

As long as I walk the earth,
As long as there is breath in me.
And when my trek on earth is done.
In Crossing, I find you waiting on the shore
More beautiful, more precious than before
That's what love does,
That's the sweetest part.

❧

Forward

*"Instead of grieving because it's gone.
Smile because it happened."*

This writing grew out of the journals I kept during my deepest sorrow of losing my dearest friend, the love of my life, my hero, my husband, Wilfred Harder, who came into my life at the age of 15 and remains in my heart until the end of time. After a 3 year courtship, we had 48 wonderful years of marriage. Through all the high roads and the bumpy ones, too, we grew more in love, more connected to each other than we ever dreamed. Together we cherished a love that stretches into infinity.

Wilfred, best known as 'Will', loved life, enjoyed people and set out to learn about anything and everything through whatever means available. He was a self motivated scholar with a passion for knowledge. His extraordinary qualities were revealed through his determination to accomplish what ever he set out to do with the best of his ability. He left his mark of distinction on the work he did, a man with strength of character and integrity who never settled for less than his best. To those who knew him, he will not easily be forgotten.

He wore many 'caps', even as he filled, with love and dedication, the roles of provider, husband, father, grandfather, councilor and friend.

From the day I found myself alone for the first time in my life, I discovered that writing letters to him was therapeutic. I poured out every part of my grief onto those pages, flooding them with tears, crying out in anguish. I came to realize that I could bestow honor on him by remembering the joys he brought into my life and others. It's those joys I wish to share as I tell our story.

Prologue

Suspending Operation

*Blessed is the man who perseveres under trial, because
when he has stood the test, he will receive the crown of
life that God has promised to those who love him.*
~James 1:12~

The whirr of fans stirred the hot August air around the
living room, otherwise so still and humid, one could barely
breathe. Birds softly ruffled their feathers as they sought to
cool themselves in the shade of a lilac bush just outside the
open window. Sadness cast it's gloom on every face as we
watched this man we loved so dearly. The man, who was
once so strong, so filled with vitality; who once loved and
comforted us through our own life pains. Now is struck
relentlessly by the flailing sword of the invisible black
demon called Cancer. Everything possible had been done.
All we could do now was stand by and offer comfort and
prayer through the occasional outcries of intense pain that
mercifully lasted only a few moments but seemed endless.
With each thrust of the demon's dagger, our hearts cringed,
begging God, *"No more. No more."* Yet, when the seizure

passed, he would open his eyes and with a weak smile, say "Thank you, Jesus." Throughout his illness, whenever he felt the stabs of pain that he knew God had seen him through, those were the words you would hear him say, over and over again And with the smallest kindness someone would pay, he would always say, "Thank you or bless you, you're so good to me."

Soft voices were heard as loved ones gathered around the bedside offering tender blessing to their beloved father and grandfather. They had arrived, in response to my urgent call, for this was the time we needed to come together as a family.

Mike and Chris sat next to the bed, one holding the hand of his beloved father , the other, his hands on his arm. Lorna and Lisa stood there too, I sat on a high stool next to his head as we intermittently spoke soothing words, adjusted his pillow or administered sips of water to his dry lips. Love poured over this room as our hearts, filled with joys and sadness for memories and pain communicated quietly among us.

Father, Grandfather and Husband, all represented in this man who lay valiantly fighting for his life. Father looked into the eyes of those circled around him, expressing his love to each of his beloved children. He reveled in their comforting presence; how precious each one was to him. With each one, he shared a special connection. The same was for their spouses as well. He cherished each one.

Grandfather proudly gazed at his grandchildren; some now grown with whom he'd shared many sweet memories together; some much younger and one more on its way. He touched each one as if to seal a blessing upon them, then seeing the youngest playing quietly on the floor across the room he asked for him to be brought closer. Lorna, gently sat her little son on the bed so Grampa could take his tiny hand in his. Very quietly he gazed deeply into the child's eyes before his mother put him down again.

He clasped hands with each one, telling them how much he loved them. Though words were difficult and sometimes almost too soft to hear, he spoke love to each child. After a while he twisted his hand loose from his son's grasp and with a weak smile he said *"Gotta, hang up now."*

So bitter-sweet were these moments with my family together again for perhaps the very last time. The battle was closing in. Now, as he gazed into the eyes of his loved ones he spoke, *"Suspend operations."* Knowing how he loved reading Tom Clancy spy novels, Mike and Chris understood what he was saying. As he looked around and was able to see each of his children hanging on every word, he asked permission to go.

We caught our breath. The thought tore into our hearts like a knife. We all expected it, yet the very sound of his request caught us unprepared. How could we bear to give him up? How could our life go on without him? Yet denying him the blessing of release from the pain and suffering would be cruel and selfish.

Together, Will and I had prepared for this time. Yet no one can ever really be ready. We prayed for this time never to come. I looked into the eyes of my beloved husband as he looked deeply into mine, the wife of his youth. I could not answer him; my lips could not form the words. Mike quickly responded with, *"It's ok Daddy, you can go. we'll, catch up with you later."* Making sure he heard Mike correctly, he asked again and Mike repeated it, reassuringly.

Talking became more difficult and then his tired eyes closed. All was silent. Chris read from the 23rd Psalm. Someone began softly to sing Will's favorite song, *"Amazing Grace, how sweet the sound"*. Others joined in.

We stood there, barely breathing as not to miss anything; thinking, expecting… perhaps this would be the moment his new journey would begin……..when suddenly his eyes popped open wide. Looking around and with a twinkle in his eyes and a slight smile, he said *"Well, now, what do we do?"* Laughter splintered the tension as we felt relief and enjoyed this treasured sense of humor with him. This was so like the Will we knew, to lighten the intensity of a serious moment with a dash of wit. Perhaps too, he was a bit surprised, that after saying his 'goodbye's' he found himself still here.

Once Upon A Time

If my children and grandchildren were to ask me where it all began….

I can recall the freshness of the moment, the details of our beginning as if it were yesterday. After all, I have replayed them in my mind repeatedly over the many years since they happened. Those precious memories live in my heart forever.

So listen, my children. This is a story that bears hearing and repeating. Everyone loves a fairy tale. This is my very own. This fairy tale actually came true for me. My 'happy forever after' journey with your father and grandfather will last until the end of time.

This fairy tale begins as many do

⚬

A wistful-eyed little girl lived with her parents on a small wheat farm in far away Kansas, who dreamed of one day meeting her Prince Charming.

In the midst of a vast prairie land, often used for grazing cattle, stood a large barn, a house and a few out buildings.

A few acres of cultivated land was set aside to raise crops. In the middle of the 1940's, with no electricity, no telephone, just a well and pump, some 100 yards from the house for our water supply. Town was seven miles away and no close neighbors. This is where we called home.

I was the youngest child. The little 'princess'. This is my story.

I was not aware of my royalty until many years later, when I met my Prince Charming. But I'm jumping ahead.

I had two brothers who adored me, and were grown when this story begins. My sister, Helen, was already married and had a daughter of her own.

I did not have beautiful satin dresses or sweet lacey petticoats like one would expect a princess to have. In fact, if you were looking for a princess, you would not have recognized me at all. I was a skinny little girl with long straggly hair. One might even consider me more of a Cinderella, than a Princess. My dresses, all homemade came below the knee. One nice one for Sunday and the faded, worn ones were to play in.

My mother washed and saved chicken feed sacks that came in brightly colored, patterned fabric. Out of these she made clothes for herself and me.

While other girls wore white stockings and cute Mary Jane shoes to church, I wore brown oxfords that were 'serviceable' and 'practical'. In the winter time, I had to wear long brown stockings to keep my legs warm. They were fastened by garter clips to a little harness that mother made.

Shy and accustomed to playing by myself, most of the time, my imagination conjured up things that I could imitate from the grown-up world around me.

I had a wagon that played the part of a car. Kneeling with one leg inside the wagon and pushing with the other, using the tongue as a steering wheel, I drove for *'miles'* around our yard. It was my Cadillac, my Buick, or what ever I wanted it to be. I rarely went anywhere on the farm without my 'car', with my faithful dogs following along beside me.

When I wasn't playing with my wagon, I drew roads in the dirt, all over the yard. I dug crevices in the ground for a river with bridges to cross (*I never could get it to hold water*). Where I lived, there was rarely anything but flat terrain, but somewhere in my limited world, I'd fallen in love with scenic roads that had lots of curves and dips and steep hills, lots of rocks and covered with trees that hung over the road from both sides. I improvised beautiful scenarios for my imaginary travels. With a little rubber car about 3 inches long, I drove those roads to 'familiar' places, or on long vacations, even to 'California'. I drove that little car until it lost it's wheels, even the running boards disappeared... finally it barely resembled a car.

In my imaginary travels I drove the 'fanciest' car, I wore the finest clothes, lived in a beautiful mansion. I was a princess.

Aunts are suppose to be old, but I was only three when Darlene, my sisters daughter was born and I have no memory of time without her in my life. Every opportunity we had to be together, she would have her doll, and along with mine, we would spend hours acting out our fantasies of living in a mansion with our beautiful children and our charming prince's.

Our relationship was like that of close sisters. Although we lived miles apart and saw each other on rare occasions. We shared our dreams and deepest secrets, just as sisters do.

We played 'wedding' , using old lace curtains to make bridal veils. We pretend our prince charming was coming on his white horse to marry us. We played this game every time we were together and never wearied of it. Ironic that the name I chose for my 'husband' was Bill.

My brother, Ralph married when I was six and served in the Army during World War II. He was away on overseas duty for what seemed an endless time. During this time, his wife, Billie gave me a lot of attention. She wore such lovely things and would often give me old purses and high heel shoes. Sometimes she even gave me face powder and perfumes to play with. I spent untold hours alone pretending I *was* a princess. Dreaming of being grown up like her and copying the way she walked and talked. She became the role model that steered me through my years of growing up.

I wanted so much to have some high heel shoes to play dress-up in. Some that actually fit me. Just like Billie wore. One summer I found a pair in the thrift shop, but my mother wouldn't let me have them.

So, I improvised. I drew the outline of my feet on the back of a cereal box, cut them out and glued a empty thread spool on to the heel. Then I wrapped it onto my feet with ribbon or string, whatever I could find. I proudly pranced around in them, feeling very grown up. Unfortunately, they didn't last long. When they wore out, I would just make another pair. I guess, my mom saw how important it was for me, because one day she did buy me a pair of *real* 'second hand' high heels that really fit. I was overjoyed….until, she decided they were just too high and worried that I would turn my ankle or something, so she took a hack saw and chopped off half of the heels.

Ray, the youngest of the two brothers, my hero, was all of 9 years older than me. He was tall and handsome. To me he was always a grown up. He looked after me, protected me, teased me and loved me. I idolized him and I think it is safe to say, I was the apple of his eye. I dreamed that one day I would marry someone as wonderful as him.

When together, Darlene and I vied for his attentions and I remember so clearly her saying, "I'm going to marry Uncle Ray when I grow up." To which I fiercely responded, "You can't! He's mine! Besides you're not suppose to marry your uncle!"

Ray showed love for me in so many ways. One memory stands out above the rest. I had fallen from a horse and broken my arm. Because my mom didn't have confidence in doctors, they took me to a Swedish Massage a few hours away, who put it in a sling and told me to exercise it every day. Their limited experience with doctors traces back to the old days when a woman named "Mrs. Faedrou" who lived in their community. They believed she had a special gifting to heal by massage or special brews.

I endured some weeks of noticeable pain and discomfort. When the swelling went down a bone projected under my skin. So my parents conceded. By the time they took me to a real doctor and had X-rays taken, the bones had grown together. I was admitted to the hospital for surgery.

Christmas was approaching. The night I returned home from the hospital, my brother Ray had a special surprise for me. When we entered the house, he told me to stay in the kitchen for a little while. At last, he came to get me and led me into the dark living room. There I saw the most beautiful lights I'd ever seen…. on a *real* Christmas tree! We didn't have electricity. He had cut the tree and purchased some real lights that he wired to a car battery. I still have those lights. Never before did we have a *real* tree. Each year before, we put up a little tree that had sparse branches of twisted green dyed feathers. It was always hung with Christmas candy, a few very old ornaments and real candles clamped to the branches to light for a short while as I sang "Silent Night". But a *real* tree made this Christmas seem like magic!

I was 10 when he fell in love and married Betty. Betty loved me too, and I would go visit her from time to time. She began teaching me to cook, or we would often embroider tea towels together and talk. It was such fun and she never made me feel as if I were just a little tag-along kid. She had a quick sense of humor and I drew on her values and personality, adopting some for myself.

The World Around Me

Our community employed many German prisoners. I'd overheard adults tell horrifying stories of war. I associated these men with them and I was afraid that would happen… here…to us.

Sometimes, during harvest, I would go with my father into town to deliver a load of wheat to the elevator where it was collected and sold. While I waited in the pickup, one of these men stopped by and spoke to me in German. I could not understand what he said. It was a disturbing experience for me and I immediately told my father. But he smiled and told me, the man just said that 'he had a pretty little girl at home just like you and he missed her'.

I can still recall the fear of hearing the airplanes as they flew in formation over my home, sometimes as many as a dozen or more at a time. We would run out and watch them fly low enough that you could see the landing wheels and read the logo on the plane. I was so afraid they would drop bombs, but these were American planes doing their practice maneuvers.

There were specified times we had to turn out all the lights and pull the shades. Cities too, were blacked out, as a civil preparation measure in case of enemy attack.

Whenever I became afraid, I would snuggle down in my mothers lap and listened while she quietly sang songs of Jesus and told me, *"Jesus watches over you. He counts the number of hairs on your head and will not allow one hair to fall without his will. He even protects the little sparrow and you are more important to him than a sparrow."* Picturing Jesus' fingers going through and counting my hair, seemed a bit hard to imagine, but it comforted a frightened little girl.

For a little girl of 6 years, many things along the long secluded stretch of road from school to home were very frightening. Most of the time, I had to walk it alone. I would run past an empty old house, terrified nearly out of my skin. Feeling a haunting presence behind me, I ran, fast as I could. I looked behind me, making sure "it" was not following me.

A little further down the road Texas Longhorns were grazing in a pasture. When they saw me, they became curious. The big herd came thundering toward me, bawling loudly, with dust flying in the air, their heads lowered and charged the fence to watch me. How vulnerable I felt with only four measly wires between posts that separated them from me! I ran for my life, heart in my mouth, arriving home with tears flowing down my cheeks. The next day, I would face it all over again.

Eventually the cattle were moved out of that pasture. New neighbors moved in close by and this gave me company on that long walk to and from school. They had a horse to ride to school. We became fast friends and each morning they came by to pick me up on the way to school. There were 3 of them and I made the 4th! Me, on the tail end! Soon they put together a cart that was pulled by the horse. This was such fun…safer too.

I was very timid. Since I had rarely played with another child accept for Darlene, it was difficult to make friends at first.

Mother had made me pretty new dresses from her stash of feed sacks for school. I quickly observed that other girls dresses were much shorter than mine.

My hair was nearly always braided and tied up on top of my head. I had no ribbons, no curls or pretty barrettes like the other girls wore.

I wanted so much to look like the other girls in school and I pleaded with my mother. She had an old curling iron that she heated on the stove and made curls for me, but sometimes the iron got too hot and singed the hair. This left my hair all frizzy and smelling like a cat with it's tail on fire. Going to school smelling like that was embarrassing. Some times she wrapped my hair with rags the night before so I would have long curls.

My hair became a daily struggle for me. It wasn't until a few years later, when I was 12 years old, Billie took me for my first visit to a beauty shop. Strange looking machines and funny hoods that fit over your head stood on one side of the room. I was lead to a chair that lifted and swiveled next to a big sink where I got my introduction into the smells of perms and lotions and the rite of hair beautification . After that, she taught me how to roll my own hair and keep it looking nice.

Although the first year of school was very hard for me, by the second grade I learned to make friends. I was able to convince my mother that it was important to me how I dressed. I wanted to 'fit in'.

Although other girls wore pants to school, my mother would not allow me to. She didn't want me looking like a boy. Finally, when I was in the eighth grade, I was the oldest girl in school. I was going to compete in a multi-school track meet. For the first time, I got to wear a pair of pants that she picked up at the second hand store but I *had* to wear it under my dress! I suppose that was acceptable as sometimes girls wore pants under their skirts in the wintertime to keep their legs warm. It didn't hinder my activities too much though. I won a blue ribbon for the 100 yard dash and a red one for a broad jump.

Growing Up

Boys began noticing me. I liked that. They began seeking me out at recess. I felt very grown up and loved the attention. Three in particular, would sit with me, send me notes, sometimes even give me little presents or stuffed the box with "I love you" cards to me on Valentines Day. They were all younger except for one. He had been held back a year. The other two were in the fifth and sixth grade. I didn't matter to me. I enjoyed their attention.

My father drove kids to and from school that year. One day, one of the boys had some notes that I had written to him. He and a couple of other boys began scuffling over them and to keep the others from grabbing them, he threw them out of the car window. My father stopped on the way back to pick them up and was quite astonished to find them written by me! They were innocent little notes saying things like 'I love you too'. You know, things like that.

When we got home that evening, he and mother sat me down to talk. Very seriously my father asked me what this 'love affair' was all about. I was cornered! I was embarrassed.

They asked a lot of questions and it took a while to explain my way through that one.

Later, in the summer, one of the boys called. When my mother answered the phone, he asked to speak to me, but she told him I wasn't home! I was quite shocked as I was standing right there and she told him I wasn't! She lied! To protect me, I'm sure, but….long before, I'd learned the hard way, never to lie! Now my own mother……?

He called a second time and I answered. He wanted to take me to a street dance in town, but when I asked my mother, I had to tell him she wouldn't let me.

~

Like most other girls, from the time I first became interested in boys, I dreamed of "falling in love." What "falling in love" really meant, I had no idea, except what I'd observed between my brothers and their wives. I was already experiencing a 'special feeling, they called 'puppy love'. Not to be confused with 'real' love, I was told.

A new phase of life was opening up for me. A time of exploring my feelings and the values I'd been taught. I had questions. Lots of them. My mother was clearly not the one to share those kind of things with. But, since my wonderful sisters-in law were great listeners and were easy to talk to about these new adventures, I turned to them. They were always ready to answer my questions. They told me, for now, I should just enjoy the attention and the feelings that rose from it were normal. I should guard my body and allow no one to disrespect me. In time I would learn more about relationships.

~

None of my siblings had finished high school. Each one had stories of going for a while, but lack of transportation, being needed to work at home, or sometimes, just not a strong enough interest, prevented their attendance. Somehow it didn't rate the highest priority with my parents who lived their lives in simplicity, believing that hard work, a little dirt under the fingernails and a strong belief in God were the basis for a good life.

Before she married, my mother taught first through eighth grade in German school in the Mennonite community where she lived. My father gave up going to school in the fourth grade. He was 16. His attendance had been so sporadic due to his need to work on his father's farm that he was embarrassed to be in the same grade with much younger kids.

In telling his story to me, he often joked, "when I got big enough to spank the teacher back, it was time for me to quit going." So my father had the opinion that if he could get by without an education, so could anyone.

My mother is the one who believed otherwise and began pursuing a high school education for me. However, they were not desirous that I should go to the public high school in my home town of El Dorado. "After all," she'd say, "there is so much evil influence in those schools." "No, it must be a Christian school," she insisted.

After much discussion and counting costs, my parents sacrificed a great deal to send me to a Christian high school. Berean Academy was 35 miles away. It was certainly too far in those days to commute, so I lived with other girls on campus.

It must have been a hard decision for my parents, my mother in particular, to see me go away. I was their 'baby' and they wanted to protect me. There was the generation gap between us that often created friction. I was struggling to be a part of a different world than theirs. Their ideas collided with mine. I was eager for the opportunity to go away to school. As all parents do, they wanted the best for me. But it was hard for them to let go.

Coming Into Bloom

Berean Academy was located in a very small rural town in the middle of a Kansas farming community that was governed primarily by the local Mennonite churches. The students who lived a distance from school stayed in a dormitory and came together for congregate meals in the cafeteria.

Many of us were new to this atmosphere. Freshman, I was to discover, were considered the lowest rung of the social ladder and were looked down on by the upper classmen. However, in the dorm there were senior girls who graciously took us under their wing and helped us adjust.

The room I shared with two other girls was small and crowded. Being raised alone and now sharing such close quarters resulted in some major adjustments for me. We shared one small closet, one dresser, 3 beds, one of which was a roll away. Very little floor space was left.

These girls grew up in a Children's Home in Nebraska and were accustomed to dormitory style living and sharing common possessions.

Georgia was petite, quite pretty and had lovely dark hair. Very quickly I was to learn of her contriving ways of using not only myself but others for her benefit. She sort of took ownership of whatever was in her grasp. She was one, I quickly learned, to keep an eye on.

Edna, large and frumpy, was not accustomed to frequent bathing. Neither one cared where their clothes landed. They possessed lot's of them, all hand me downs, but in spite of them not fitting too well, they were suitable. My own wardrobe was adequate. Nothing lavish or fashionable, but it fit in. I had a few things my mother had made, but for the first time in my life I had some that were purchased new. Imagine my shock when I entered my first class, to find Georgia wearing some of *my* clothes! The nerve!

"Oh" she said, with a perky little toss of her shoulders. "I didn't think you would mind." I did mind. I made it clear I did not appreciate this game and would not be playing.

"My mother", I told her sternly, "scraped and saved to provide these clothes for *me* and I am not sharing them with you or anyone else."

I quickly made other friends. Just prior to the beginning of school I was notified that my roommate for my freshman year would be a girl named Jean.

My parents and I meet her and her parents. We began making plans. But it turned out that Jean would be driving to school, instead, and we would not be roommates after all. This was disappointing to both of us, and perhaps that was the catalyst that brought us together.

Jean was charming. A delightfully witty girl. We took a quick liking to each other. She made me laugh and I loved to laugh. What fun we had. She wore the cutest clothes that her mother made. They looked just like store bought and I envied her.

It seemed that it came easy for her to talk to almost anyone. Still there was a shyness about her. She had grown up in the same community as some of the other students and some were even relatives. Some held themselves above others and did not appreciated her sense of humor. But Jean had a way of overlooking their bad behavior and enjoyed life.

She became a trusted friend. It did not take long before we formed a real bond and shared our most valued secrets with one another.

❧

Our time was closely regulated outside the classroom. The dorm students were not allowed to leave campus without permission from their supervisor. Our comings and goings were under close scrutiny. A long list of regulations kept us accountable. Boy/girl relationships were monitored closer still. No chance of getting into mischief there. "No bodily contact, please," was often heard from a faculty member passing through the crowded halls where couples were walking hand in hand.

I had matured a lot during my first semester at Berean. I'd even had a boy friend or two for a short period of time, but suddenly they would become disinterested. I watched relationships develop and crumble. It seemed strange to me that relationships would come and go on a whim. Sometimes without a word, just a cold shoulder. Suddenly neither one could find words to speak to the other, almost as if they were embarrassed to have been friends at all.

Some guys I observed seemed to behave so immaturely, often treating girls with little respect. I began to form some definite opinions about the quality I wanted in a man. My man.

When First I Saw Him

The students had just returned to boarding school after the Christmas holiday. We were assembled in the auditorium at Berean Academy, where Jean and I were sitting near the front. We were busy chatting about our holiday while we waited for assembly to start. Rumor had it that a new student had come and we wondered who it could be.

Suddenly, my attention was drawn to several boys on the other side of the large room who were engaged in some laughter and teasing.

And then,

I saw him.

He wore a daring black leather jacket. I'd never seen a boy wear a black leather jacket. His blond hair was combed into a deep wave over his forehead. His eyes laughed like a blue summer sky in my winter. He seemed to be the center of attention in this group of young men as if he were the prince in his court.

My breath caught as I nudged Jean to look over and then I saw other girls leaning forward to see him too. Secretly, my heart was already laying claim on his.

For the rest of that assembly, I heard nothing, saw nothing....but the handsome new guy across the aisle. My mind was consumed with thoughts and pictures of myself in the company of this young man.

There was a unique persona about him. I knew, because I watched him, day after day. I watched as he walked between classes from building to building with an unusual spring in each step, as if he had places to go and was happy to be going there.

Compared to the other guys, he seemed confident, mature, courteous and friendly. I didn't see a boy. I saw a man. He lived in the boy's dorm across the campus from me. He was a junior and his name was Wilfred, but his friends called him "Fritz." He sported a raccoon cap like a mountaineer might wear, proudly displaying his origin from the mountains of Idaho.

Some of the girls began hanging on his arm and begged to wear his cap. I wished I could wear it, too . It quickly began to appear that every girl wanted a piece of him. Including me. But I was too shy, and my old fashioned up-bringing had taught me that it was not proper for a young girl deliberately to demand attention from a guy. She should wait and let him make the first move. Oh, I really wanted this guy to notice me…. Oh, if only he would! I wanted to wear his cap. I wanted him to carry my books. I could think of nothing else. The 'love sick blues' kept playing over and over in my heart. I spoke of my hopes only with my dearest and most trusted friend, Jean.

I believe, I began loving him even then, but I reminded myself, that a man of his distinction surely would not be interested in a silly freshman. Besides, I couldn't bring myself to flirt with him in order to win his attentions as the other girls did. Doing that would lower my standards and that wasn't who I was. Even if I did, I was afraid I would loose my chances with him.

Mean while, Georgia, my drama queen roommate, as I began to call her, was at work with her beguiling ways. She knew exactly how to get what she wanted, and when she spotted Wilfred, she immediately set her stakes on him and trapped his attentions.

He seemed like such a nice, sensible guy and I wondered how he could be so blind not to see her for what she was. Poor guy, he fell for her and I was crushed.

Then I began to wonder just what kind of guy would fall for a girl like her, a little floozy who boldly flung herself at any male. She played him like a toy and when she spoke of him she showed little respect. Did he know that? Maybe he wasn't so smart after all. Maybe I should just forget him. But I couldn't. Whenever I saw him with his arm around her, I felt a stab of pain. Night after night, she would gush over him in our room. I did not want to hear it. I wanted to strangle her!

For the rest of that year, I followed him with my eyes, but sure that he was lost to me forever. At this point, I think I began to see myself becoming an old maid. At 14?

Getting To Know You

September 1951, students returned to school, eager to make a fresh start, renew friendships of last year and discover new ones. The atmosphere was filled with excitement as everyone was eager to exchanged their summer epic's and catch up on the latest news.

I had not forgotten the young man in the black leather jacket. My heart had carried his image all summer long. I could not get him out of my mind. When I learned he was back and no longer attached to anyone, hope was restored. Perhaps I had a chance that one day he would notice me.

Over the first weekend of school, everyone had been busy getting settled into their dorm rooms, but at the first breakfast of the year, I caught a glimpse of him as he came into the dining room with his friends. I couldn't believe my good fortune when he chose to sit at the same table as mine. Not a word was spoken, but I remember carefully watching my etiquette, fearful of spilling 'the sauce' on myself or doing something else embarrassing. My eyes avoided his. Just being in his very presence, satisfied my appetite.

The bell rang for school to begin, everyone was crowding and bumping into each other, intent on getting their books and finding their classes. I stood by the office door, waiting for it to open so I could get some information about a class that I was to take. I looked up.

There, before me were the most magnificent blue eyes I'd ever seen. I felt a flush surge through me as our eyes met. I blushed deeply and lowered my eyes.   Suddenly, my head felt as if it was soaring somewhere high above me. It was Wilfred! Shyly I stole another look and saw his eyes were still fixed on me. This time he spoke! I can't remember what he said. But, for the first time his words were directed at me. My heart pounded wildly. I lost focus on everything else but him.

Only a few brief insignificant words were exchanged. The office door opened for business and we went our separate ways. Yet the sound of his low, soft voice, echoed in my heart all day.

Little had I known that while he was seeing 'that' girl last year, he had been watching and admiring me. As I discovered later, neither did he know that I had been secretly watching him too. Had he been thinking of me all summer, as I had been thinking of him? He said he had.

One day, as I grabbed my books out of my locker and was heading out the door for my next class, he stepped forward out of the crowd and with a voice like warm honey, he asked me, "May I carry your books?" Was this really happening? I had dreamed of this moment, thinking it was out of reach. Now, this handsome young man in the black leather jacket and sweeping golden hair was walking beside me. The one that all the girls wanted! And he was carrying *my* books. My head floated on clouds. I was afraid to speak or even look up, lest this glorious dream would end. But he broke the silence by making trivial small talk. My mind could not grasp it all.

We shared a Spanish class. Wilfred and his buddies sat on the back row, playing funny Spanish word games, teasing the teacher and making everyone laugh. I withdrew from any interaction, barely opening my mouth for fear I would embarrass myself *and* him.. Consequently, I didn't learn very much Spanish; I wanted to join in the fun, but I was too shy to bring myself to try it.

He began waiting after every class for me and at meal time he was there to escort me to a table where we would sit together. Simply being in his presence gave me such a feeling of euphoria. What ever the opportunity, we caught each other in a glance and we would smile. Our conversations began to come easily in our eagerness to learn more about each other. When I would dare to look into his beautiful eyes and see his looking back at me, I had to pinch myself to see if this was real. Me, of all the other girls who were more beautiful, more popular than I was, he wanted to spend time with me.

Basketball season began. Will tried out for a cheerleading position and wowed everyone with his forward flip in the air before landing solidly on his feet. This was most impressive to us girls and we never missed a game. There were three cheerleaders. Two girls, wearing blue skirts and white sweaters, waving their pompoms and then there was Will. Boy, did he look good in his white pants and blue shirt, turning his somersault in the air! They waved their blue pompoms and cheered our team on to victory. But mostly I saw Will; I was so proud to be his best girl.

❧

Christmas time arrived. The holiday spirit escalated as the time drew closer. It also cast a shade of gloom over me.

We would all go to our respective homes for a two week holiday. That meant Wilfred would be going back to Idaho. I wasn't sure I would ever see him again. Would he even think of me ?

I was in class when he had to leave to catch his train, but he left a gift of perfume and a sweet note for me with one of his friends to pass on to me.

One day during the holiday, I received a postcard with a picture of beautiful Idaho mountains. It didn't say very much, but it was signed "Love, Wilfred." This was the first mention of 'love'. I read it over and over. My soul devoured it. My heart soared. Already, I knew the sound of his voice and I repeated those two words over and over to myself imitating that same low voice so it sounded like him saying them to me.

After we returned to school from the holidays our relationship eagerly picked up where we left off and began to flourish. We spent much of our time on campus, together. Nearly every evening we sat together on the sofa in the dorm. He told me about the big snows in Idaho and about the mountains; that the roads were closed while he was home for Christmas, so he had to ride 6 miles, on horseback, to and from the post office in the bitter cold to mail the postcard he sent me. That sounded like 'love' to me!

At the end of January, winter came with a vengeance. The bluster of snow, hard winds, and very cold temperatures bore down. Winter colds paid visits to the students, one, two or three at a time. I was one. I was so sick, I couldn't even go to meals, so someone brought them to me. Will began sending sweet little notes with Jean, saying how much he missed me and signing them "*with love*"! Every evening, I could look forward to one of his notes; the best medicine I could have had.

Those of us students that lived on campus in dormitories were required to attend study hall each evening after supper for two hours. Because it was considered a class, we had to follow the same rules of classroom behavior, but we somehow managed to make it as unstructured as possible. It all depended on the faculty member in charge. Some were more relaxed than others. Study hall was held in the library, so we were free to wander around the room. Occasionally, Wilfred would get up and walk around so that he could keep an eye peeled on me. When our eyes met, he would wink at me. Oh, that wink! It drove itself deep into my soul! That wink would turn my whole body into jelly, take my breath away and leave me longing for more. Still for a time, I was very cautious, afraid I would scare him away. Yet when I saw him, my eyes lit up and my heart beat accelerated. I couldn't help myself. But, always, I gave him my best smile and shyly lowered my eyes, in hopes of encouraging him.

Somewhere along the way we had begun holding hands when we were together and soon after that his arm reached around me as we sat on the sofa or walked together. I savored each moment, every touch, every word he spoke. We spent many hours, talking in the reception room of my dorm. Sometimes he would scoot very close to me and even try to kiss me, but I would shyly move away.

One evening after Will walked me 'home' to the dorm, and we were saying 'good night', he said to me, "I bet you a nickel I can kiss you without touching you." Since he had already tried to kiss me a few times, and hearing this now, I knew he was trying to trick me. Laughing, I slowly shook my head and told him "No-oo…you're just teasing me." I knew he really wanted to kiss me. That was obvious. But, always the gentleman, he respected my wishes, yet, he used any cute ploy to persuade my inner longings.

After that evening, every time he passed by me, he would jingle the coins in his pocket and wink. Each time, it would send an electric current through my whole body. For the years to come, for the rest of our lives, no matter where we were, that wink remained our secret communication and spoke a 'loud' "I love you" across a crowded room. That wink never lost its magic.

Discovering Love

We began spending more and more time together, our friendship grew, we were more comfortable with each other and our conversations took on a deeper meaning. We would sit hand in hand or with his arm around me and talk for hours without running out of things to say. We told each other about ourselves, our families, our dreams, our interests, singing little songs to each other or sharing ideas about anything that came to mind, including what we expected in a marriage relationship. Never had there been anyone for either of us that we could share such intimate thoughts with, nor have such understanding and trust.

My 'dorm mother' kept a close eye on us. Miss Wiens, an unusual person, worked at being graceful and proper, but she had a slight tendency toward clumsiness. We girls often thought her to be a bit weird and spoke of her as a typical *'old maid'*. She wore thick glasses that accentuated the size of her eyes and her hair stuck out to the sides in a wild natural curl. She could spot those who stretched their 'luck' to the limit and we all knew we could not escape her 'evil eye'. When she laid those eyes on you, with an ever so

27

slight frown, you knew you'd been had. But in all fairness, I can't remember when she didn't use wisdom in her actions, even though at the time, we often thought differently. Still there was something endearing about her.

Occasionally, she called me into her office to council me on my relationship with Wilfred. She became concerned about the amount of time we were spending together and suggested, "Maybe you should take up some other activities. Perhaps ping pong or tennis." But, even though she kept a keen eye on us, she often looked the other way.

I sometimes think she saw what a special bond Will and I had. Wilfred had gained the respect of all the instructors by his respectful manner and maturity, so I believe we may have earned extra favor with her in particular.

◆

It was a chilly night in late February. The snow had disappeared by now but a cold North wind remained. Study hall was over, we were left quite undisturbed, now that most of the students that lived in the dorm had already made a speedy dash against the harsh wind to their rooms, for a nice hot shower and warm 'jamies.

Will slowly walked me to the dorm, under the clear brilliant star lit sky. The brisk wind whipped around us, but all we felt was the closeness of our bodies and the warmth of our budding love. We stood inside the entry saying good night to each other. Will looked around to make sure we were alone. Then he pulled me into his arms for the first time to hold me very close. I, in turn, closed my arms around him. For the first time, I felt his passion as he pressed me firmly against his body. The nudge of desire lit a fire that burned through us both. I stayed in his arms in perfect stillness, while feelings awakened in me, so new they left me quivering and breathless. A bit embarrassed, I thought maybe I should pull away, but I didn't. I couldn't. I pretended I didn't notice. I wanted more, yet when he found my lips to kiss me, I pulled away. Oh, I wanted so much for him to kiss me, yet I wanted to savor one wonderful discovery at a time. I would not let myself.

We didn't speak of these moments for a while, but the next time he held me and for all the times after that, our hunger for each other deepened. Our conversations took a more intimate turn as we recognized we might be falling in love.

❖

On a particular Friday evening, there was a special event taking place at a church several miles from school. Since my parents always came for me on Fridays, we agreed to meet there. I had been looking for an opportunity to introduce Will to them and this seemed to be the ideal time.

My parents were cordial to Will. After chatting for a short while, I told them, "I still have to go back to the dorm to pick up my suitcase. Would you mind giving Will a lift back to his dorm too?"

They agreed, but this surprise hit them quite unexpectedly. They had assumed I had brought my suitcase and would be going straight home with them.

Later, they chuckled at how I'd had that all planned out, but the warnings began.

More from my mother than my father. First, "You are way too young to even think of such things.' 'You can't possibly know what love is about,' or 'you can't possibly know what your doing'. "There are many other fish in the sea," she would say. "Don't settle for the first one that comes along." and " Don't accept any jewelry of any kind from this boy." The list seemed to go on and on.

Lies, Road Muffins, and Scandal

There were several girls that tried to steal his attentions. He was a real catch. But this time, his eyes were on me.

My roommate, Sadie had lost her mother some years before and seemed to have no one, so I invited her home for weekends from time to time and my mother took her under her wing. Most of the time we were pretty good friends, but from time to time she would tell me tales that were meant to discourage me of Wilfred's interest.

For Easter Sunday, with my mom's permission, I invited Wilfred to come have dinner at my house. He didn't have his own transportation, so he would be coming with his cousin, Johnny. We arranged that Sadie would come home with me for that weekend and she and Johnny could meet. Lots of excited planning went into this anticipated visit. Sadie and I went shopping for new outfits together, helped my mom prepare the dinner and eagerly awaited the big day.

On waking, early Easter morning, I was not feeling so well. I tried to ignore it. Nothing was going to spoil this day!

But within minutes I noticed red spots forming on my body. When my mom saw it, she said "Chicken Pox!!" I knew in my heart this day was ruined.

When she told me I would have to call Wilfred and cancel our visit; my heart broke. It was so hard to tell him not to come. We were both so disappointed and I cried. All the dreams and plans for this perfect day, were now shattered.

Sadie did not take this well. She thought it improper that I cried when I called to tell Wilfred not to come and told my mother so. Sadie was angry. Angry at me for spoiling *her* day, angry for losing her opportunity to meet a new guy....just plain angry. My father had to drive her back to school and I was left behind to recover. From that time to the end of school, she began spreading false stories about indiscretions she imagined of us.

Spring was in the air and some of the 'farm' students were feeling adventuresome and rode their horses to school. This created a commotion that went far beyond the fun it was intended. Naturally the horses left 'road muffins' on the side walks. Lots of them. That's what horses do. When the school custodian, a man in his 60's, saw this, he became very upset. Becoming irate, he began running after the equestrians, wildly waving his arms and yelling angrily at the boys at the top of his voice, "This is a Christian school! This is *not* the way to behave!" As if the horses knew it wasn't Christian to crap on the sidewalk?

Wilfred was watching and he walked up to the man. As respectfully as he could, he said, "Sir, it seems to me that a Christian should not lose their temper at such a little thing." "Just give them a shovel. They will clean it up." For a student to reprove him, really set his temper blazing, and the custodian immediately reported this impudence to the Superintendent.

Word spread quickly and during the next hour class, Jean, told me to brace myself. She had heard, "Wilfred has been accused of being the leader of a shoplifting ring." That was an outrage! I refused to believe her, but within a couple of hours we were all called back into chapel, where it was announced that Wilfred was being suspended from school, along with 3 other guys who had been caught for shoplifting. He was sentenced to a 3 weeks suspension. The shoplifters got only 2 weeks. Wilfred was placed into custody of a local relative where he would do hard farm labor. The incident with the custodian was never mentioned. I knew Will was not a thief and tried to talk with him, but his accusers had whisked him away before I got a chance.

He was denied any kind of contact with me for the three weeks period. I was devastated. I knew that he was innocent, but I was not even given the opportunity to tell him that. How cruel, how unfair they had been to him! He left a note for me saying he was innocent of the accusations and during the suspension his friends delivered frequent written messages that we wrote to each other. Soon, a personal motto was phrased between the two of us, *"When there's a Will, there's a way."*

⌥

Some weeks later, Will was cleared of any shoplifting involvement. This came, after Will's father demanded a public apology from the school board, some of which were relatives of the family. However, it wasn't until the evening of graduation, that the president of the board came to shake his hand (which he did with all the graduates) and made a slightly apathetic apology to Will. Guess that was better than nothing.

One weekend when I was at home with my parents, Johnny brought him for a visit for the first time.

On expecting his arrival at the appointed time, I'd made sure things in the house were in order and my personal appearance was at it's best. I eagerly watched, expectantly out of the window that faced the drive. When I saw the car approach, I took one last look around the room and gave one quick glance into a mirror. My breath caught as the car stopped at the front gate. Breathlessly, I waited until the gate closed behind them and they came to the front door......

I opened it.

Both of our faces glowed with the joy of seeing each other and for that instant we were lost in each others eyes. My parents were right there to express their welcome to my guests. We sat in the living room for a short time and made polite conversation, while Will and I just wanted to go somewhere and be alone.

Soon Johnny dutifully suggested the three of us go for a drive to the El Dorado Lake. Finally, away from my parents, Will and I could embrace. At the lake, Johnny found a lovely shady spot near the water and we sat there all afternoon. The three of us talking and laughing, while I sat snuggled into the comfort of Will's arms.

Sometime later, Will told me, "That Sunday when I saw you come to the front door to greet me, a sudden feeling came over me. As if I'd seen you once before when I was a kid. At my cousin's wedding. I was told 'if you put a piece of wedding cake under your pillow tonight, you will dream of the girl you will marry.' Then seeing you Sunday, that same feeling came over me. As if you were that girl in my dream....and I knew.."

Commitment

On a lovely spring evening we sat on the foot scraper outside the library, watching the stars and talking together. We were alone. Just the two of us. Will looked at me and asked " Do you believe a man and a woman can still be in love as we are and build a life together, even if they are separated for three years by miles and time?"

My breath caught. I was speechless as I pondered that question. By now, I was quite sure what I felt was real love. I understood what he was saying. Graduation would be in a few short weeks and I still had two more years of school left before I was finished. There was also his college or military ahead. Already I could not imagine life without this man.

Turning to look in his eyes, I said, "Yes, I believe they could."

I knew he was talking about us, but I had to ask myself, *'How could I know that far down the road? Was I really ready to make such a commitment all by myself?'* I was only 15 years old. Soon I'd be 16, still considered too young to make a choice of such magnitude. Always before, I had asked someone else for advise. Yet, as I viewed our relationship, I considered what we had together. Knowing he would soon be going away, perhaps forever, I could not let him go. We had already committed our hearts and now it was time to make it verbal.

At this moment, he took my hand and led me inside the school building. Pulling me into a dark corner under a staircase, away from everyone, he took me in his arms and held me close. His face was so near, I could feel his warm breath. Then holding me back so he could look into my eyes, searching, hopeful, he asked, "Will you marry me?"

I did not know what to say. I stood there searching his eyes for a moment, my heart was crying *"yes, yes"* but my lips were mute. I could not speak.

Sensing my hesitation, he pulled a quarter out of his pocket and said "Shall we flip for it ?" "Heads we get married, tails we don't?"

That was a chance I was willing to take, not even giving it a thought that it could possibly come up tails. Without a doubt in my mind, I expected it to come up 'heads'. Thank heaven, it did! " Heads" he called! We looked at each other and laughed. I knew the answer in my heart and I said, "Yes, yes, I will marry you!"

Slowly, he drew me tighter to himself, and lowered his face as I raised mine to meet his. Very slowly, his sweet smooth lips covered mine in our first breathless kiss. Our hearts melded together in that moment, our love for each other was sealed for the rest of our lives.

I knew then that I loved this man and wanted to be with him forever. Neither one of us had any doubts about this commitment we were making. Will was the most honorable man I knew. It would be unthinkable that I could let him go. I believed in him and would place my trust in him for the rest of my life.

Little did we really know of what loneliness we faced. What lay ahead would be the greatest test of all. One thing we did know, our love was strong and it would only grow stronger. We would make it happen.

A relationship of this significance should consist of the journey
From friendship, to passion, to enduring love.
For the path is one of testing
For through dark opposition, distance and betrayal,
Love is refined

❦

I shall never forget the day. It was my 16th birthday. The dorm was already alive with activity. I bounced out of bed, and dressed quickly as I was eager to go down to the dining room for breakfast, where I knew he would be waiting for me. Relishing the thought of his special attention on my special day, I swept into the cafeteria anticipating his lavish welcome. But…to my dreadful disappointment, Will was not there. He and the other seniors had all fled in the wee hours of the morning for their 'senior sneak'. I understood that this was traditionally an annual occurrence and no one was to know when it would happen. But, how could he not have told *me*? My heart was broken. For an instant I thought this was a bad joke, then I ran from the dining hall back to my room. I threw myself on my bed and wept.

"Why could you not trust me to keep a secret? I thought you loved me! If you really loved me, you would have shared your confidence with me! Especially today. Today is my birthday!"
and now it was the worst day of my life.

I could not understand why he hadn't trusted me with his secret. That was the worst disappointment of all. In the years to come, I would learn that Will's word was sacred to a fault. If he promised to keep a confidence, his lips were sealed. I would come to appreciate his trustworthiness, not only to me, but to everyone who knew him. But right then, in that particular situation, that moment, my heart was crushed and alone.

How could I possibly get through this day? My mind was not on school work. I choked back tears and somehow I managed to get through it.

I didn't go down for breakfast the following morning. I stayed in my room, trying to face the day ahead of me. Trying to think what I would say to him when I saw him.

Someone came to my room to tell me I had a visitor. It was Wilfred! I splashed cold water on my face and ventured uncertainly into the sitting room where he was waiting. I entered the room, my eyes still red and swollen from crying. He saw my pain. He didn't have to ask.

He took me in his arms and tried tenderly to sooth my wounded feelings and assured me he had not forgotten my birthday. He tipped my face back and looked into my eyes. He was sorry for disappointing me and was telling me again how much he loved me. My pain was still very fresh. My eyes again filled with tears as I saw his sincerity. I wanted to forgive him, but….

Then he reached into his pocket and pulled out a small box and placed it in my hand.

Still tearful, my breath caught as I opened this little box. My heart stopped. I could hardly believe my eyes! I had not expected such a gift! But there in the little box, shining up at me was the most beautiful ring I'd ever seen. My heart was pounding wildly as I watched him slowly take it out of the box and slip it onto my finger.

Then he said to me, "I want you for the rest of my life. This ring is a symbol of the promise we made to each other and to seal the commitment of our love. One day there will be a real engagement ring to announce our up coming marriage, but for now this ring will hold us through the rough time ahead. "

Instantly, my world lit up. I wore that ring so proudly to classes that day! Word spread quickly. Everyone was excited for me and had to see the ring. Excitement and pride had over come me so that I did not even think how my parents would react.

❧

My parents would undoubtedly be shocked to learn that my relationship with Will had become serious. Mostly because I was so young. They'd had a couple of brief meetings with Will but, they didn't know him.

I was afraid of their reaction. How could I possibly tell my parents that I'd already given my heart to Will? That we were planning a future together; that we were in love? I should have braced myself. I was not adequately prepared for what might come once I showed them my ring. I understood that it was not an engagement ring, but to them, that's what it would look like.

But, by the time I got home, I was overcome with eagerness to share my excitement. I was too excited to wait. I held out my hand for them to see my birthday gift from Will. Instantly, my mother reacted in disbelief and shock.

"How could you do this to me? What were you thinking to accept such a gift from a boy you hardly know?" "You have to give it back." "I warned you about such a thing." Why, why, why?

"But I do know him, mom." I said. "I love him. We have spent weeks, months learning to know each other,"

She listened to nothing I said. Daddy on the other hand, said very little. Looking back, he was pretty cool about it all.

My heart was on a run away train and these pleas from my mother did not deter me. I would follow my heart. I trusted this man and I gave my heart freely, without reserve. I couldn't wait to get back to school after the long, miserable weekend at home, to cry on Will's shoulder.

He suggested I take the ring off, but I would not do that!

Years later, I could see her reason for being so concerned when our own daughter appeared to be steering in the wrong direction. Parents are entitled and given the responsibility to direct their children and forewarn them of possible road blocks ahead.

In my case, I was so young and they hardly knew Will. In hind site, I know it was unfair to spring this information on them like this. I should have told my parents about him much sooner, but I was afraid of their criticism. I knew what I wanted and didn't want to risk their disapproval.

She did not trust Will. A man she had barely met. Someone who would come and rob her little girl out from under her wing. Mother didn't trust men in general and she certainly did not have any faith in my judgment. Mother never really spoke to me about the qualities to look for in a man. She would only warn me against them. Now her warnings were void. My heart was taken.

During those following days, it was a relief to be away at school, away from my mother's critical censorship. Allowing me to revel in this new euphoria.

Graduation

Our time was growing short. His graduation was just around the corner. On occasion the school bus would take a group on a field trip. We were never allowed to sit together, but usually Will would take the aisle seat just behind me and we would hold hands around the corner. This satisfied our need to touch, to talk and feel our love pulsate through each others hands.

But, I was 16 now. Sixteen was the official dating age at school, which meant we were finally allowed to take long walks off campus together. Sometimes we walked to the cemetery outside of town, or anywhere we could be alone for a while. A place where we could talk. We spent nearly every waking hour that we were not in classes together.

Graduation day finally came. It was a tearful time for both of us, knowing we would be parting for an indefinite time. Will introduced me to his parents who had came from Idaho to attend his graduation. They seemed very nice, but all I could think was, they will be taking him away from me.

It was mid-afternoon and the early June air was soft and warm as we took our last walk out of town. But the ominous approach of the graduation ceremony, to begin in just a few short hours, overshadowed these wonderful moments we would spend together. As we walked, arm in arm, we shared our dreams, our love, our hopes. We made promises to each other, not knowing when we would see each other again, yet believing some day in the far distant future, we would be married. We tearfully held each other close. An eternity was about to separate us, but this had to be enough for now. He was going back to his home in Idaho, so many, many, long miles away and I had to stay behind and finish 2 more years of school.

We walked along the road, with our arms linked around each other, taking in the essence of being alone together one last time. Then I asked him to reach deep into the huge pocket my mother had sewn into the new pink skirt I was wearing.

Eagerly, he reached down and pulled out a small box with a ribbon tied around it. As he opened it, his delight over the handsome pair of gold cuff links and tie clip was expressed with sweet hugs and kisses. I'd saved the money to go to an exclusive men's store and bought it without my parents knowledge.

After the graduation ceremony, while I hung on his arm, he bade goodbye to his many friends. After the final farewell were made, he turned in his cap and gown and we were free to be alone. We went to his parents empty car and once again, I lay tightly embraced in his arms. We cried. We repeated our vows of commitment, our love, and promises of far off tomorrows and we cried some more.

Then his parents came and announced it was time to go. Painfully, with breaking hearts and tears streaming down our faces, we gave each other one last lingering kiss goodbye.

Sobbing, I retreated to my dorm room, desiring a few moments alone with my sorrow.

Instead, as I entered my room, I was greeted by a chill. My mother and Sadie had been engaged in a serious talk, that abruptly fell silent on my entry. Whatever they were discussing seemed to be aggravated by seeing that I had been crying. Their scowls conveyed their distain and tension filled the room. I clearly would not have time alone. I busied myself packing the rest of my things to take home, while a sense of dread overshadowed the summer ahead.

It was a long silent trip home…..

The Scarlet Tale

It was some time before I learned what had really transpired in that room, prior to my arrival. The days that followed were torturous at home. I was missing Will with my whole being and my mother was acting as if I had totally dishonored her. She lay on the couch, clearly in deep depression or ill. I didn't know which. When I asked what was wrong, all she could say was, "you should know." But I knew nothing. Mom would not look me in the eye or talk to me. Whenever she attempted to speak, she started crying. She continued this for a number of days. I thought perhaps she was sick, but she said she wasn't. I could only guess then, that it had something to do with Will. But what?

One evening, after about a week of this, while I sat at the table after supper, she walked by me and slipped a brochure to me and kept walking into the next room. Imagine how astonished I was to find this brochure was information from a home for unwed mothers in Texas! I couldn't believe that she would think I was pregnant! After reading it a couple of times I confronted her.

"What is this all about? Do you think I'm pregnant? Why would you think such a thing about me?" Question after question tumbled from my lips. I was shocked and angry. I didn't know what to make of this!

❧

Jealousy had pierced Sadie's heart so deeply that she could not stand to see me happy. On one other occasion she had already cautioned my mother about my 'behavior' but on *this*, the most heartbreaking night of my young life, Sadie betrayed me. On that very night even as Will and I were saying our tearful goodbyes, not knowing when we would ever get to see each other again, she was filling my mothers ears with lies. Lies! She told her of our walks off campus into the country. Indicating she was sure she knew what we'd been up to.

"Sadie told me I need to start making baby clothes," Mom said, accusingly.

I sat in silence with my mouth open and eyes wide. Speechless. The words reverberated in my ears like the clanging of an empty tin barrel.

"......and," my mother continued, "haven't you missed a period??"

"Sadie lied to you, mom!" I resounded, repulsed.

"But why would Sadie say such a thing if it were not true?" she asked.

"And you would believe her word over mine? Mom!" I cried

How would mom know that I'd missed a period? I certainly had not told her. I didn't know why I was late. To tell the truth, I hadn't even thought about it. More important things had been on my mind. Certainly it had not been priority in my thoughts, and it definitely was not the reason she assumed.

But trying to convince her was out of the question. I tried to assure her that Will and I had not been intimate. He was a good, virtuous man. We had agreed to wait until we were married. He honored me, but she would not listen to a word I said.

I'd never seen a doctor alone, but that week I made an appointment with one privately. I told him about Will going away and what mom was putting me through. He assured me that missing periods was not unusual for young girls. While the hormones are trying to regulate themselves, and sometimes due to the trauma of the past few weeks, the cycle would be disturbed. I was not to worry and gave me a shot to get me started again.

I suppose that reassured my mother a little, but, she couldn't leave the issue about the ring alone. The ring was very much a thorn in her side, and to her it only represented a threat of loosing her daughter. To me, the ring was a symbol of everything beautiful about the love Will and I shared,

We told each other everything in our daily letters. I poured out my heart to Will. His reply was prompt, begging me to throw the ring away, far into the field, rather than live under such stress. I firmly rejected that idea. There was no way I would do that. I valued what the ring represented too much to do that. So he finally convinced me to take it off and keep it in the box. I did just that, but, on every chance I could be alone, I took it out and tried it on, shining it in the light, watching it sparkle; remembering the promise that it held.

I guess mother thought I'd given it back, because 23 years later on my last visit home before she died, she asked me about the ring that Will had first given me. I held up my hand and showed her that I was wearing it along with my diamond engagement and wedding rings.

She gasped as if shot by an arrow, "Oh, you don't mean it! I thought you had given it back to him. You promised me!" You would have thought I had betrayed her. I laughed and said to her, "Mom, I married the guy. We have 4 children."

The Long Summer

While Will was still in school and he was absent, he had slipped notes to me through the hands of some of his trusted friends. I had saved every one. In the lonely hours in my room, I would read them over and over until I nearly had them memorized. My love was 2,000 miles away. How would I possibly make it through the next three years without him? But for the promises we made to each other that we would write everyday and the commitment of our love, I could do it.

A long lonely summer followed. It was broken up somewhat by spending some of that time with my two brothers and their families. These visits gave me an opportunity to find retreat from the critical eye of my mother as they knew and understood my feelings for Will. Since I was an only child at home, this also taught me valuable lessons in child care as I helped play, dress, or feed the little nieces and nephews.

‥⊙

Everyday, at 9:00 sharp, I would start up the old Plymouth and kicking up hot dust on the lone gravel road, I drove one and a half miles to the mailbox where our road met the highway. Thoughts in the form of pictures raced around in my head with the anticipation of finding a letter from Will. Rarely was I disappointed by not receiving that coveted letter. I could hardly stand it if, by chance, a day was missed, but almost always I could count on there being two the next day.

My heart stood still as I approached the mailbox. On pulling opening the box, my eyes focused for only one thing, that familiar handwriting in green ink. I snatched it up as if it would disappear before my very eyes. Safely in my hand, I could feel that healing balm surge through me as I held it to my breast. As if it washed all the tensions of my life at home away and soothing my yearning heart.

As I got into the car, oblivious to the intense summer heat beating through the windshield, I ripped the envelope open. Immediately I could feel his arms around me. I could smell his after shave. I'd scan through quickly till I got to the 'good stuff', then I'd slowly reread the letter before turning around to go back home. Once, home again, I'd rush to my room and read and reread the letter over and over, listening to the memory of his voice, as he told me how much he missed me and loved me.

For nearly 3 years, we continued, day after day, sharing our thoughts and dreams for the cost of a 3 cent postage stamp. You can do the math, but the price of true love has untold value.

There were always the customary late summer projects. Helping my mom store up peaches, apricots and 'blue' plums for the long winter months ahead. Making pickles, picking green beans and canning them seemed like an endless task.

Without running water, having to carry it so far, then boil it on the stove in the smoldering heat of August gave me reason to never, ever want to do that myself. School would not begin any too soon for me.

❧

Finally the day came to fill the car with bags of clothes, bedding, and personal items and head back to Berean Academy. Being a Junior in high school gave me a feeling of maturity. Jean had been my dearest friend for 2 years now, and from the time we'd first met we had desired to share a dorm room together, but it hadn't worked out. She lived several blocks away on the other side of town, so it was to her and my advantage to spend nearly every free moment together in and out of my room on campus. There we did homework together, just talked or cooked up some mischief to get into. There was never a dull moment with Jean around.

My room mate didn't mind, as I rarely saw her. She had other friends she hung out with and in the evening before bed, she would wait until lights were out to undress for bed. She had an attitude of superiority. She considered herself to be a better Christian; a more dedicated student, and more sophisticated than us. Jean and I saw her as 'stuck up'.

She remained aloof all that year and the next.

❧

School was already in full swing when Will and his parents came to Kansas for a visit. I was given permission to miss a few days of school while we spent that time together at my parents' home. This presented the opportunity for our parents to meet and have dinner together. A time to get acquainted, and I'm sure to talk about their "lovesick" kids.

My brothers and sisters made a special trip on the weekend to meet this guy they had heard so much of. Their approval held utmost importance for me and I wanted him to know them too.

They all tend to be a loud bunch with lots of teasing and offering opinions. It was important that he see them as they are so I tried to prepare him. They did not disappoint! Betty, Ray's wife, loved to have fun and had a great idea how to break in this new prospect. If he could pass the test, he was *in*.

Dinner was on and everyone was called to the table. Will and I were placed on the side of the table next to where Betty would sit. Knowing Betty, she had planned it that way.

Will proceeded to sit down, but, he quickly came back up with a surprised look on his face! Wondering just what he had sat down on, he looked behind him…then laughter erupted while he scooped up the remains of a hard boiled egg. Holding it in his hand he looked around to see just who might have placed it there. But the glisten in Betty's eyes revealed the secret. Immediately, he tried to give it back to her. They scuffled for a brief moment and the ice was broken. He was *in*! One definitely had to be a good sport to fit into my family.

❧

Foreseeing, once again, the dreaded separation that was eminent, Will tried to convince his parents to let him stay and attend college in Newton Kansas, but they would not allow it. He was needed on the farm.

Saying good-bye once again, left me feeling empty and alone. I went to my room and threw myself on my bed, sobbing until there were no more tears. But, going back to my friends and the routine of school helped get my mind on other things.

Each day after school, Jean and I walked downtown to the post office to pick up my letter from Will. I could tell that the postmaster had something for me by the way the he always lit up when he saw me coming, Just before he handed it to me, he liked teasing me by telling me that a letter had not come, but his eyes let me know differently.

By pulling some mischievous antics, sleeping over and spending weekends at each other's homes, the year passed amazingly fast.

A Sack of Idaho Potatoes

Between my junior and senior year, I had another lonely summer to face. I'd just turned 17. With every letter, our loneliness grew more intense. Our longing for each other was tearing us up inside. How could we continue to live without each other?

One day my parents got a notice in the mail that some freight had come in their name. Curious, my father went to the freight station in town and to his surprise, it was a 100 pound bag of potatoes from Aberdeen, Idaho. A timely act of kindness as potatoes were a rare commodity that year and very much appreciated.

A letter from them followed the next day, along with a train ticket and invitation for me to come visit their potato farm in Idaho! I could hardly believe it! I was so excited! But, would my mother let me go? Would she even consider it? Will had been to my home several times now and her confidence in him had slowly begun to develop. After much discussion and trusting that his parents would be present at all times, to my amazement she and my father agreed. I could go!

My mother pulled some fabric from her stash and began sewing a few things I needed. I counted each day to the time for me to go.

At last the day came when they drove me to Newton, about 60 miles away, to catch the train. With a verbal list of warnings during the entire drive, they put me on the train. At long last, I was on my own, for the first time in my life!

The train was waiting. Ready to embark on this amazing journey, I heard the porter call *"all 'board"*. Then he took my hand and helped me up the steps to the train car and I found my seat. I heard him call out, *"all 'board"* once more. Then the wheels began to grind as I felt the train slowly pull away from the station. Everything seemed surreal. Could this possibly be me traveling to Idaho? Alone?

The long train made it's way slowly, winding through the Colorado Rockies and Wyoming sagebrush. Occasionally, it stopped to let off or pick up more passengers in some small town. Watching from the window I observed mountains, and countryside I'd never seen before. Mile after mile, listening to the iron wheels pounding on the rails and the car rocking slightly to and fro, an occasional whistle from the engine filled my ears. I pictured myself once more being in the arms of my true love. Mother had packed sandwiches for me to eat while in route. I had never been on a train before and found everything fascinating. The ladies restroom was large enough to change clothes in. The porter, dressed in a handsome uniform, passed through our car from time to time, calling out the next stop, or offering sandwiches and drinks from a cart.

It was July 19th. Midnight of the second day. Just in time to help celebrate Will's 19th birthday. My train pulled into the station in Pocatello, Idaho. The porter tapped me on the shoulder and told me I had reached my destination.

Joan Saner Harder

My heart was racing as I gathered my things and prepared to disembark. Oh, what indescribable joy, to see my love waiting to catch me in his arms. Even, now, 50 some years later, I still can feel the thrill of that reunion.

Before he drove me to his home, in the little town of Aberdeen, 50 miles away, he took me to eat in an all night café. While we waited for our order of hamburgers and fries, Will fed some dimes into the jukebox at the end of our table. We listened to our favorite songs. *Via con Dios, The song from Moulin Rouge, Unchained Melody* and others, played as we talked and soaked in each others eyes.

It must have been almost dawn when we arrived at his home. After giving me a brief tour around the house to acquaint me with my new surroundings he cut a slice of chocolate angel food cake his mother had baked for his birthday. After sitting in this strange living room, sharing his birthday cake, we said our good nights and went to bed. Will would have to get up very soon to irrigate the field.

As I began to settle into the room I would occupy, I observed the smells of this unfamiliar house, and the simplicity of the room I was in. Not so unlike my house back home. I studied the tiny patterns on the wall and a vintage trunk that sat against one wall. I wondered what secrets it held of by gone days. My mind was so full of the past few hours of our reunion, it was a while before I could fall asleep. But the occasional creak of the otherwise still house, the sound of an owl hooting somewhere outside and hearing the birds as they were beginning to waken in the early pre-dawn hour finally lulled me into dreamland.

It seemed only like moments later, I heard a tap on my door. Will was back from the field. He tapped on my door to see if I was awake and asked if he could come into my room. I couldn't wait to see him and invited him in. I had been sound asleep and still in my pajamas. The ones that my mom had made for me of sack cloth with little girls in pigtails all over it. We held each other close as we consumed as much of each other as we allowed. We talked and kissed and savored the precious moments we'd waited for so long. Our hearts beat together with love and passion for each other, yet, we knew our limits and respected them.

This is *Idaho*

His parents had been in church that Sunday morning, but we were downstairs by the time they got home, ready for the dinner his mother had prepared. Then Will took me for a long walk around the farm, showing, explaining all the processes of irrigating their potatoes and sugar beets; so different from just waiting for the rains to water crops in Central Kansas.

There were mountains on the distant horizon, fields of crops and sage brush that grew up everywhere it could. The smell of sage brush filled the air, the soil was a gray powder that filtered into your shoes with every step. I found what I saw of Idaho to be oddly beautiful. Definitely unique, from the pasture graze land in Kansas.

Will showed me his personal shovel he used for irrigating and the wooden handle he had carved our initials into. WH loves JS "Makes the shovel work so much better" he told me, with a wink. I still have that shovel, though the letters have faded.

In the evening he took me to a rocky hill west of his fathers barn and across a wide irrigation canal, to show me a spectacular view of the lake beyond and the lights of the city of Pocatello working their way up on the mountains in the background. It was a beautiful view. We watched the lights and the stars glistening on the water just a few feet below us. As we stood there, our arms wrapped tightly around each other, Will told me of his dream of one day building a home for us in this very spot.

We spent many hours in the pine room he had built when he was younger. We found it amusing when he showed me a letter he'd received from my mother just before I came, begging him *'not to crush her little violet'*. His mother had also expressed to him her concern about our spending so much time in his room, but whatever he said to her, seemed to put her at ease. It was basically the only place we could be alone and comfortable, except for the times we would go for walks or drives.

Will's mother suggested we go to the "Nat" to swim, but again, my mother made me promise, before I left. I would not show myself in a bathing suit……. So many rules.

He couldn't wait to take me out to the desert where he loved to hunt rabbits. Sage brush covered the landscape for miles to the west, intermittently scattered with lava rock. Equipped with two hand guns and two rifles and some instruction of their use, he placed one in my hand and pointed at a couple of long ears hiding in the sagebrush just ahead.

"Now, hold the gun steady and find the spot just between the rabbit's ears through that little sight at the end of the barrel." he said, quietly. "When you are ready, hold it real steady and pull the trigger." I will never forget the instant the bullet hit and down went the rabbit! How proud he was when I shot this rabbit ….dead! On my first try! I couldn't believe I did that and he couldn't stop telling everyone what a great shot I was. Pure luck, I was sure.

At night he would drive me to the lake to watch the moonlight form a "bridge" over the water. One day, we drove to Scout Mountain on the other side of Pocatello. I'd never been into the mountains before. As we drove upwards on the winding road the pine trees grew thicker as their aroma grew stronger. We stopped at a clearing to eat the picnic lunch Will's mother had prepared for us. Suddenly, a bee tried to fly up my skirt. I jumped up and screamed in terror. Frightened, the bee flew away. While Will calmed me, he had to speculate what he would have done to save me!

His parents took us on a day trip to Jackson Hole, Wyoming. We sat in the back seat, absorbed in each other when we were not taking in the magnificent scenery . Will rented a motor boat so that he could take me across Jenny Lake to the foot of the beautiful Grand Teton.

I'd never in my life seen mountains like we saw that day. Such an amazing sight! Looking up at those majestic peaks, it seemed as if they were rising straight up out of the water, reaching into the heavens, far above us. I could barely comprehend what I saw. What enchantment! I'd never been on a boat before, either. Unfortunately, the motor quit in the middle of the lake, so Will had to row all the way back to shore. He told me stories as he rowed, never letting on the effort it took.

Later that day, Will told me he had lost 'our' magic quarter over-board when he visited the "out house". The quarter he had flipped the year before to see if we should get married. Well, I guess, we were sure enough of our decision, that we could laugh about where it was lost and that he had no desire to go after it. Still it seemed a little sad that our special 'token' was lost never to be retreived.

Will's parents were very cordial. His mother, a soft spoken woman, treated me graciously, making sure I was comfortable. Yet I couldn't be sure what she thought of us together. Was she just being polite? I couldn't tell. When Will took me to his brother's house to introduce me, they too greeted me pleasantly with a brisk handshake.

We attended his church together once and met a few of his friends that were still around. Their handshakes, too, were a strong single pump of the wrist that I presumed to be characteristic of Mennonite people. I tried to imagine myself fitting into this picture.

The farm...well, that seemed easy enough. My home and farm were not nearly as big. Their home seemed to have a few more comforts. A bathroom, for one. But, everyone seemed so formal. So unlike Will. The atmosphere was comparable to that of his relatives in the Whitewater, Kansas area. Definitely a Mennonite trait, I surmised. But, I was so deeply in love and didn't give any of it much thought.

This delightful time would soon have to end...but, for now we would store up as much magic as we could for the lonely times ahead, when our separation would become harder and harder.

We could not get enough of each other. In the months and years to come we would be ripped apart, again and again. We never ran out of things to talk about or laugh about, and sometimes cry about. How could we ever survive the loneliness, we wondered? When would the time come when we never would have to part and we could be together forever?

It had been the most glorious two weeks of my young life. Like a dream. All too soon, the time came. We heard the last call, "All 'board". One more hug, one more kiss before I tearfully boarded the train, again. With one last wave *"good bye, my love,"* we watched each other disappear as the train slowly carried me out of sight. Back to Kansas. Back to more loneliness.

Will Goes To Chicago

The Korean war began in June of 1950. A few of Will's acquaintances had already gone to serve overseas. Since he couldn't go to college, he felt it was his duty to serve his country in the military. When he presented this idea, his parents profoundly rejected it.

They had come from a long line of pacifists, a belief that violence, even in self-defense, is unjustifiable under any conditions. There would be no discussion in this matter. He would be following in the principle of his forbearers. A few religious groups concurred to this belief, particularly the Mennonites. He did not feel inclined toward that conviction, but to honor his parents wishes, he agreed to enter 1-W service.

Young men from pacifist backgrounds who do not enter the military for religious reasons are given alternative service to perform. One of the two capacities of alternative service is called noncombatant which (classified 1-A-O) serves in the Army without using weapons or handling ammunition. The other is classified as 1-W Service and they do civilian work contributing to the maintenance of national health or safety, often in hospitals like the Veterans Administration. This was the choice Will and his parents made.

Soon after, he signed up for a two year term and was sent to North Chicago, where he and other men in this same rank served as orderlies in the Vets hospital. One of the men, happened to be my cousin, Jerry from South Dakota. Another, was engaged to marry my cousin from Minnesota. That connection meant a lot to both of us. I had never realized until then how small our world could be.

Will's job was to keep order on a ward of mentally challenged veterans. This assignment kept him on his toes every moment. He sometimes broke up fights or escorted patients to meals or doctors, played pool or cards with them and at other times supervised them on trips to movies or major league ball games in Chicago.

It was his job to make sure the patients on his ward were showered and prepared for bed. One of them proceeded to dress himself and Will noticed he was putting on a pair of ladies underwear. Will told him this was unacceptable, and wanted him to take them off. He refused, so Will tried to take them from him, when the patient hauled off and punched him…in the face….and broke his jaw. Years later, our children remember hearing his jaw pop every time he ate steak!

After the first year, he had the opportunity to work as a surgical technician along side my cousin Jerry, from South Dakota. Will enjoyed the work and found surgery fascinating. He and Jerry, as technicians were responsible to keep the surgical room, scrubbed, sterile and ready at all times. During surgery, they circulated, assisting doctors and nurses with whatever they may need. They were also in charge of washing the rubber gloves, blowing them up to check for leaks, powder them, package them and send them through the steam autoclave to be ready for the next use.

They rolled, wrapped and sterilized bandages as well. Even the injection needles were sharpened and reused. Now, a half a century later, it sounds strange and unsanitary to us.

They were on call, alternate nights and weekends for emergencies. When their call came, they would drop everything and get to their job as quickly as possible to take care of their duties.

They developed a good rapport with the nurses and doctors and enjoyed the friendly discussions that took place between surgeries. Many interests were shared together during their work hours. Some of which drew Will into a new world of possibilities that inspired him to considered a career in nursing or physical therapy, but that never developed. He later considered phycology. But by that time, we had a family. The opportunities always seemed just out of reach.

The professional staff became interested in the reason Will and Jerry were working there. During their slack time, when they had time to talk, they asked about pacifism and the Mennonite church. This also lead to conversations of other churches, and other beliefs. Will began learning about other people's views on God, religion, and life. These discussions and reading numerous books from various perspectives gave Will reason to consider the differences. He began wondering just where he fit into the picture. Who was right; who was wrong? Was Heaven real? Or Hell? Was God real? These questions led him on a 20 year search for answers that would satisfy his keen intellect. At the age of 20, this quandary led Will to pen these words:

Thirteen Steps to Hell
Thirteen steps to the big oak chair,
How you wonder if you'll make it there
You think of Satan at the gates of hell

Ten more minutes, and you'll be there
The warden comes to your prison cell
And tells you it's time to go.
The chaplain prays, but you know good and well
That it's only thirteen steps to the gates of hell.
You take the thirteen steps to the big oak chair,
The chaplain walks beside you till you're there
Five more minutes and you'll be down there.
They strap you down to the big oak chair
One electrode on your leg, the other on your head.
You think again of the gates of hell,
Two more minutes and you'll be there.
One more minute, the warden raises his hand,
The executioner stands with his hand on the switch
The warden drops his hand
There's a terrific jolt …and…
Your in Satan's land.
-Wilfred E. Harder-

Celebrating Our Engagement

We had seen each other so little since he left school. Each time, it became harder and harder to part. Computers and E-mails did not exist, telephone calls were very expensive, so we wrote letters to each other every day and still the time seemed endless. Every day I would check the mail to get my letter and what a thrill it was to open it. I devoured every word as nourishment to my heart. Through those letters we discussed every thought, poured out our love for each other, shared our dreams, and learned to understand the deepest part of each other.

In those letters, I could feel his breath in every word, the warmth of his arms around me and his heart beating with mine. Perhaps that is why our life together stayed so strong. Even though we were so young, we believed in our love and our commitment was sacred. We were willing to do whatever it took to build a life together.

In May of 1954, 2 years after Will graduated, he came for my high school graduation.

The day of graduation, Will asked me, "Do you still have the ring I gave you for your 16th birthday?"

I said, "Of course, I do" and eagerly opened my dresser drawer to take it out.

I handed him the box, but he told me, "Open it."

When I opened the box, I couldn't believe my eyes! This was *not* the ring, he'd given me 2 years before. In it's place was a brilliant diamond ring! I was stunned. Overjoyed beyond words. Once again, he took the ring from the box and as he slipped it on my finger, he sealed it with a long embrace and kiss.

At last....a real engagement ring! We were officially engaged! The moment we both had waited for.

He had come prepared and had already asked my father for my hand in marriage.

My father liked Will. He could see what a fine, sincere man Will was and believed he could entrust his baby girl into his care. So with my fathers approval, I could proudly wear this beautiful diamond ring for all the world to see that our engagement was official.

Will always treated my parents with honor and respect. My mother's disapproval lessened and I think she secretly came to like him. Particularly because he listened to her disapproval with respect and constantly assured her he loved me with all his heart and wanted to take care of me for the rest of our lives. He would do whatever it took to keep me from being hurt.

With each visit, he gained more of my mother's confidence. Although still skeptical, she was agreeable. But, she reminded me that as a child I had told her, *Mommie, I will never leave you."*. With tears in her eyes, she sadly said, "If you move far away to Idaho, I'll never see my little girl again.." Even though she did not express happiness for us, she gave her consent on the condition we wait a year to marry.

I proudly wore my new engagement ring to the graduation ceremony that night. Only Jean and a select few had seen it so far. Throughout all the pomp and ceremonial speeches I heard very little; my mind was whirling with excitement as I watched the blinding sparkle of the stone as the light reflected from above. And once it was noticed, the word spread like wild fire, all my friends crowded in to see and congratulate us.

Those who were not my friends, simply had to see to believe. Some declared *"it'll never last"*.

The rest of my family came to see me graduate and to see Will again. They liked him and expressed their delight when we showed them my ring. They were well aware of our feelings for each other and eagerly began congratulating and teasing us on the announcement of our engagement.

Will and I had never been on a 'formal date'. But he asked my fathers permission to borrow his car and invited me out for dinner to celebrate our engagement.

This was officially my very first date and with the man of my dreams! How exciting it was to be dressed in our very best. I, wearing my new diamond ring and the dress and shoes I'd purchased for graduation. Will was in his suit and tie, and wearing the tie clip and cuff links I'd given him on his graduation.

He took me to the 'Polar Bear', a lovely restaurant in Wichita. We were ushered to a quiet table set with candles, a table cloth, and cloth napkins folded into pretty shapes between the silverware. It was so elegant. Soft music was playing in the back ground. Will knew I loved fish, so he ordered fresh Rainbow Trout.

When the waiter brought our entrée, smelling so delicious and beautifully arranged, I was not prepared for what I saw….a whole fish, smiling up at me! Two eyes met mine as I looked down at my plate! My father's favorite sport was fishing, but when he brought them in, he had already removed the head and tail before throwing them into the frying pan. I had to ask, "do I eat the head too?" Will laughed and said they leave that on just for effect. This was a fancier way to present the plate, I was to learn.

To add more romance to our dinner that evening, we were serenaded by a violinist who strolled by and stopped to play just for us. I'd never experienced such luxury. I felt so grown up….me eating in an elegant restaurant with the most handsome man in the world, my Prince Charming!

This visit went by way too fast, as had all the others, but we always made the most of them. My daddy had no hesitation about lending Will his car to court me, often making sure the gas tank was filled before we drove off. (Of course, Will always brought it back full.) Sometimes we went to visit my brothers for a few days, which we did this time as well. We always had such fun with them. Other times, Will would take me to be introduced to some of his relatives at Whitewater. But now our time was over and once again we would have to say good bye. A year seemed so far away, yet it was an absolute event to look forward to. We resolved to wait a few more months. We could do this!

The Count Down

Will returned to Chicago and I took a job working at Woolworth's department store behind the candy counter where you could buy the candy by the ounce or by the pound. After measuring it out on a scale, I put the candy into a bag for the customer. This was one of the old stores that had wooden floors and every counter had to have a full bucket of water behind it in case fire broke out, so we could douse it. Each of us employees were assigned to one counter. It was our job to keep our area clean and well stocked.

My boss could be something of a tyrant at times. So this kept us on alert, making sure we looked busy at all times I liked my job. As long as we towed the line, he could be quite pleasant. People who bought candy were rarely in a bad mood and often liked to joke and tease, so it was very pleasant. Plus, I could sample as much as I liked…. when the boss was not looking. Certain candy, *the cheap stuff*, was okay to sample from time to time, (*just to make sure it was fresh*). But getting caught eating his expensive candy, could easily result in a loud tongue lashing.

While at work, one day, I'd heard from some of the towns people that there was a raging prairie fire burning and was moving too close to my home. I asked permission to leave in the middle of my shift to go home and check on my parents. My boss threatened to fire me if I went. I couldn't stay and work, knowing my home and maybe my parents were in danger. I went anyway. Fortunately, the blaze had diminished short of our home by the time I got there.

Prairie fires were common in the graze lands and fields of Kansas. Many times, I remembered, my father and brothers would go out late at night to risk their lives to join other men from the community in fighting fires that threatened a barn or home of a neighbor. Their only weapon was to use wet burlap grain sacks to beat out the violent inferno that tore through the countryside. With a tractor or horses and a plow, a wide furrow would be cut in hopes the blaze would be stopped. No one rested until the brave fire fighters wearily returned, covered with black soot and smelling like a smoldering cinder, exhausted, on the verge of collapse. In my mind, I believe I associated this battle with that of a war. A mighty force that swept through our immediate world and left black destruction in it's wake.

When I returned to work the next day, my boss reluctantly allowed me back. But, after about six months, I quite, because Will came on the train to spend Christmas with me.

We were deliriously happy to be together again. We walked down the road from my home to cut some cedar boughs and tied them together for a Christmas tree. Then we decorated it and helped my mom prepare for Christmas dinner when the rest of the family would be coming . The snow, the festivities, the sights and sounds and the wonderful smells from Mom's kitchen made this Christmas particularly exciting with Will there.

We set our wedding date for April 10, 1955. We made plans, but waiting for those last months to pass would be the hardest of all. Both of us felt the pain and often cried together. Once again we tearfully parted, hopefully for the last time, each trying to assure the other *"only 4 months more until we are together forever."*

Christmas was over. Will went back to Chicago. I took a temporary job for the month of January and February, at the court house typing annual auto license applications. I liked the job, but it was difficult to keep my mind focused. I was so lonely for Will. Jean's wedding day was to be very soon, which made me lonelier yet. My best friend was going in a new direction in life. I worried she would no longer have time for me. I would soon be following closely behind her. but right then I could only feel the loneliness of it all. I could barely fight back the tears as I worked.

If I didn't get my daily letter, the loneliness became greater still. Will was feeling very discouraged. Our only consolation was that in two more months, we would no longer be apart…ever!

The Ultimate Challenge

One day, in late February, I received this letter from Will, expressing the terrible ache he felt. Nothing so unusual about that. We told each other that in every letter. But this one was different. He told me he didn't think he could hold on for another two months. He was going crazy with longing and he asked me to "forget the wedding plans, forget the waiting. Please come now. I desperately need you." he wrote, " Please take the next train to Chicago and we'll get married here." "I don't know how I can wait any longer."

My heart stopped at the thought of what he was asking me to do. I felt myself go weak. Was I loosing him? My whole world was turning inside out. I understood how he felt. I too wanted to be with him, more than anything, but this......, this was not just a wish. This was a plea of desperation. What about our dream wedding? What about Mom and Dad? They would be crushed! It would destroy them. I didn't know what to make of this. What if I didn't come? Was he saying 'it was over, if I didn't?' I argued with myself over and over. How could I do this to my parents! I had a decision to make, the toughest decision in my life!

Could I do this? Did I have the strength, the courage to do this thing he was asking of me? How will I answer him? He had never pressured me before and this was so private that I had nothing; no one to turn to other than my own heart.

My heart was broken. A mighty battle raged while this quandary churned around and around inside of me. I wept. I prayed. *"Dear God, what am I to do?"* How? How would I go about it? My parents… I wanted to honor them. I wanted a wedding. For so long, I'd dreamed of seeing myself in a beautiful white gown with my 'prince charming' waiting for me at the altar. Could I give all this up? Could I set my selfish dreams aside?

One thing I knew for sure, I couldn't risk loosing Will. I didn't want to give up the man I loved, the man I wanted to spend the rest of my life with. I wrestled with this all that night until I was nearly ill, but I made my decision.

Telephone calls in those days were not made on a whim. They were costly and called for desperate measures. This was certainly one of those times. Yet, I could not call from home. My parents would know and that would generate too many questions.

I stood in a daze at a phone booth on the street corner in El Dorado. Amidst the noise of traffic and the bitter wind whipping around me, I took the receiver in my trembling hand and dialed the operator. The operator told me to drop my coins in the slot while she connected me with the number Will had given me. I couldn't believe I was actually going to do this! What if he couldn't be reached?

The phone was ringing. My heart was in my throat as I waited for Will to be paged. I felt as if I would faint or be sick. I was only 18 years old, I reminded myself. I was so afraid to make this decision. My knees were weak and shaking; not sure they would hold me up. I was so unprepared. But I had no choice. I had to follow my heart. I took a deep breath and steadied myself. I would do this.

When he came on the line, I cried….we both cried. I could hardly believe it was him on the other end of the line. In between tears he told me how the loneliness had become more than he could bear and he couldn't wait any longer. I was lonely too.

Inside, I kept wondering what my parents would say or do. I knew I would have to break their hearts, but I was certain I would not break his. My loyalty was now to the man I'd promised to marry. As I stood there trembling, with tears in my voice, I gathered my strength and told him quietly, "Yes, I will come, if this is what you want. I…I don't know how, but… I will come." Inside, my heart was screaming, *"Why, why does this have to be so hard?"*

But, after we talked of our loneliness some more, he said, "Just hearing you say you are willing to do this for me helps ease the pain."

He slowly added, " Sweetheart, we are both having a rough time of it. It's only two more months. We can tough it out. The wedding plans are all made, I know how much you want this wedding. I miss you and need you so much, but I really just needed to hear you say that you loved me enough to throw it all away for me. In just a few weeks, the waiting will be over and we will finally be together for the rest of our lives. I hit such a low. I yearn for you, body and soul and I simply cannot live without you." he continued. "But talking with you now, I feel so much better. I know now that I was asking too much of you. I can wait six more weeks."

With a few more "I love you's", and more confirmation that *we can do this*, we bade our "good by's."

And we waited and planned.

I was so relieved, but my emotions were in confusion. We had come so close to a major crisis. We often wondered in years to come, what direction our lives would have taken, had we succumbed to our intense need.

Wedding Plans

My temporary job at the court house was over. Now was the time to really get busy and prepare for our wedding. Invitations to order and send out. Wedding party to choose. It went without saying, that Darlene and Jean would be my attendants. Of course I gave them official invitations. Making decisions of colors. We decided they could wear the formal gowns they wore at their graduation to save a little money.

Daily working together with Will by mail on plans for the ceremony helped us focus on the soon to be wedding.

By now, Mother seemed to have mellowed. She seemed to have gotten use to the fact that I would be marrying Will. Still, we disagreed on a number of things. She didn't want to listen to my views, so it was her way or she was out. We were coming from completely different generational views, so for the most part, I gave in and the wedding plans proceeded.

Jean's mother was making the wedding dress for her wedding, so she offered to make my dress too. Mom and I shopped for fabric and ideas, making certain the dress design was modest according to Mom's specifications..

She wouldn't come to the wedding if we didn't sit down and listen to a sermon. We compromised. We would remain standing and listen to a short one. These days it is not uncommon for the minister to give instructive words and blessing to a couple, but then the custom was 'to the alter and back out' as quickly as possible.

If we had "*I love you Truly*" sung at the wedding, she would not come…..'too worldly'. She didn't think that God could honor that and this was to be a "Godly" wedding if it killed her! We agreed on the "*Wedding Prayer*" and the "*Lord's Prayer.*" My brother-in -law, Ernie, insisted we should serve a meal or he wouldn't come. We served cake and ice cream. Mother didn't think we should have flowers. Too expensive so I paid for the flowers. I seemed to find myself at more odds than ever before in my life.

I had fun shopping for personal things I would need. I bought a gorgeous long, very sheer night gown for my wedding night. When I showed it to her, she almost fainted.

"Why, you can see everything through it!" She gasped with her hand over her mouth.

To further shock her, I flippantly replied "Yep, that's the idea."

Will's mother had an old rug on which her parents stood in a Muslim mosque, when they were married in Germany, a hundred years before. Others in the family had used it and she asked if we would use it too. I declined as graciously as I could, but I was the one to blame for breaking the Harder tradition.

Life is full of adjustments. Sometimes it's easier to compromise in order to avoid conflict. It was not easy, trying to please everyone and I quickly learned that was not even possible. Everyone offered his own ideas and wishes, even when they were not asked. But through all the hurdles, we finally came to the last week before our wedding.

After many fittings, my wedding gown was finished. My bags were packed. I was ready and eagerly anticipating the coming of my Prince.

My Prince Arrives

April 8,1955, two days before the wedding. In the wee hours of the night, I lay in my bed, unable to sleep. Waiting. Waiting for my prince to come. No, he was not coming on a shinny white horse, but he could have been. My bedroom window caught the lights of oncoming cars and I waited. Anticipating. My heart skipped a beat every time headlights beamed over the hill close to my home, but….my heart dropped every time it passed by. I prayed for his safety and begged for the next car to be his. The night grew long as the hours crawled by. I pictured our wedding day and entertained the dreams and fantasies of our upcoming wedding night.

Oh, the joy when that final car slowed and I knew that in moments he would be holding me, kissing me.

Just as the eastern sky took on it's first glow, the car rolled in. Before it came to a complete stop, I threw all modesty of the 50's to the wind. Wearing only my nighty, I jumped from my bed, and in my bare feet, flew out of the house, to be caught up in the arms of the man I loved. Dissolving all the waiting into the ecstasy of long wet kisses, he pulled me inside the car. We held each other with the fever that had built up for so long. The fire of our passion burned as he held me in his arms and we spoke of the time, so very near now, when we could yield to that fulfillment together. More passionate kisses and then – early dawn became a full glowing morning.

My mother appeared at the kitchen door, thus bringing us back to reality. There were last minute plans to make. People would be arriving soon to help with the wedding. The last minute preparations to make and in the midst of it all, we would snatch a few moments to steal away for more embraces and burning kisses.

Meeting with the pastor for a quick counseling session proved to be only a formality. An hour is hardly enough time to learn any thing needed to begin a marriage; but after all, we had been in love for three years already and didn't we know just about all we needed to know? We thought we did. We'd talked many times in our letters to each other about the many things we would face together, as we could imagine them. What more was there to learn? But, in time, we did learn there was much more we needed to know. In today's world, couples receive weeks of counseling and instruction on much needed communication skills, which we thought we had, but found later to be lacking when needed most. There was little written in the way of guidelines at that time, for a couple planning to be married.

❧

The Day before our Wedding......

April 9th. Family and close friends began to assemble in my parents yard. It was a beautiful warm spring day. The air was filled with excitement. Jean and her new husband Don, brought their wedding clothes and the four of us modeled for pictures. Just two months earlier I had stood with them at their wedding. Now Jean would be *my* bridesmaid. I was not concerned about Will seeing me in my bridal gown before the ceremony. We were secure in our own destiny; we had already spent too much time away from each other. Such a trivial tradition just didn't matter to us.

The day was filled with more busy things: chairs were set on the grass and we ate the wonderful food my mother had prepared for the large group. I met my new in-laws, some for the first time. It was hard to grasp that they would now be my family as well, but I told myself *"they probably loved Will as my siblings loved me. They would be my family too."* Will had chosen his brother- in -law, Bill, to perform our ceremony.

Darlene, my Maid of Honor, my 'dearest sister' became strangely distant as the day wore on. During our rehearsal at the church, through all the usual flutter and interfusion of putting together the perfect wedding ceremony, it became more noticeable that tears were very near the surface of her eyes. Will and I wanted so much to comfort Darlene. We told her again how much we loved her and what she meant to us, but in moment's like that there is little comfort. I recalled just a mere two months earlier, I had experienced the same thing before Jean's wedding. A sudden alienation taking place, subconsciously worming it's way into the heart and creating a void that is indescribable.

How does one explain the joyful sorrow of seeing your best friend move into a dimension we have not yet experienced? One experiences a fear of loss and emptiness for that precious friend as you realize that things will never quite be the same between you again. Your loyalties are making a major shift. How do you deal with that? How can you explain that fear? Only understanding and tears and time can wash it away. This is one of the grieving processes that takes place between best friends. Yet when the tears have dried and the fears put to ease, your loyalties are still in tact. There is an inexplicable strength in a relationship that carries that friendship for a lifetime. Not so very different from a marriage.

Everyone who was associated with the wedding, came together at the church to rehearse. Mother approved the songs we had selected. Ray had a wonderful tenor voice and it was my desire to hear him sing at my wedding. While he practiced Will and I knelt during his singing of "*The Wedding Prayer.*" Ray's precocious son Rick stood impatiently beside Will as our ring bearer. Being only 5 years old, he began to fidget so Will leaned over and whispered to him, "How's it going, Rick?" Then, with a deep sigh, and a hint of boredom he expressed aloud, "Well, it would sound a whole lot better if he sang "Davy Crocket."

This brought us all down in a peal of laughter. Nothing like a child to break up the tension of a situation.

Our Wedding Day

The morning sun shone so brightly, promising a day our dreams would come true. April 10th Easter Sunday Morning…The Long Anticipated Day of our Wedding!

I knock on Will's bedroom door. I enter and he reaches for me. I snuggle into his arms under the warm covers. This is Our Day! This is the First Day of the Rest of Our Lives! The day we will finally become Husband and Wife. The day we will hence forth be free to unleash this desire for each other that has been silenced for way too long. We savor the moment as we exchange our good morning kisses….until Mother taps on the door. She keeps a close clock on our time alone. "It's time," she calls. Time to rise and embrace our day.

My father had placed a round galvanized tub in my bedroom for what Will termed, the 'Ceremonial Bath'. We had neither running water nor a bathroom in our humble country home. Mother heated water on the stove and Daddy poured it into the tub. Traditionally, at my house, I got to bathe in the clean water, then Mom or Dad followed. In this case, however, Will got to bathe first. When it was my turn, I got a fresh tub of water.

My room was on the end of an enclosed porch, so it was easy access to the outside. I often felt like I lived in a fish bowl, as my window was next to the back door and if the curtain was open even a peep I felt exposed. But this morning, I was so filled with anticipation, I didn't notice as I soaped and perfumed and powdered to make myself worthy of the Prince who awaited me.

◦

My brother Ray was at the church when I arrived. With a familiar twinkle in his eye he greeted me with, "Well, we're off like a 'herd of turtles." I adored my big brothers. Ralph the eldest, and Ray loved teasing me and taking care of me, making sure the expression of their love kept me entertained. There was always lots of laughter between us. My brothers and their wives, Billie and Betty had given me much needed guidance and exemplified a marriage I wanted to model after.

It was time to put on my beautiful white gown, made of satin and lace. Tiny satin buttons gracing the long sleeves from elbow to wrist and the high neck to below my waist, all had to be fastened one by one. Darlene and Jean joyfully helped me while we laughed and giggled with excitement. Finally, the veil was placed on my head and a beautiful bouquet of Easter lilies placed in my hand. I was ready.

The music played while the guests arrived in small clusters and were ushered to their seats. The candelabras were lit at the alter flanked with baskets of Easter lilies. The time had come. Friends and family; the people I loved. Everyone was smiling while the minister and the groom with his attendants took their place. Then Darlene and Jean walked in. My Daddy took my arm as the tone of music changed. The *'Wedding March'* began to play. The congregation stood.

Slowly, Daddy and I began walking down the isle to the altar. My Prince Charming was waiting for me just as I'd always dreamed he would. The guests, the beautiful preparations, the prolonged agony of the past three years, all vanished as our eyes fixed upon each others.

At the end of the long walk, my father placed my hand in Will's as we drank in the moment. Our moment.

"Her mother and I do" was vaguely heard after the minister asked 'who gives this woman….'

We saw nothing but each other as we stumbled through our vows. The ceremony was quickly over. We were pronounced husband and wife. When the minister said

" Now, you may kiss your bride" Will grabbed me and gave me what possibly was the longest kiss in history. So long, in fact, the congregation began to laugh and cheer. No one knew better than us, how long we had waited for this moment. No longer could anything or anyone keep us apart. From now and forever, we were 'Mr. and Mrs. Wilfred Harder!'

❧

We stood with our parents as we greeted the guests, then excused ourselves to have pictures taken. Afterwards, the reception was held in the old church building, across the street from the new one where we were married.

The bridal party sat on a platform and were served ice cream squares and cake. There was no table. We just sat there in a semi-circle. Staged, we were, like an exhibition, eating our refreshments. I wonder now, who's idea it was to put us on such an awkward display like that?

There was no music or jubilant celebration, just the loud hum and rustle of people talking pleasantly among themselves. I remember very little about that event, other than my attendants, Darlene and Jean opened all the gifts which Will and I later viewed, and we signed our marriage license. We endured the reception out of courtesy to our guests and parents, for we were thinking of only one thing, to get away. As soon as it seemed proper, we bid our good-byes and made our leave.

I've often thought since, what an amazing celebration we should have had. We had certainly earned it after such a long wait, but……. it *didn't* happen….then. However, we spent our whole life trying to celebrate each day as it came.

I have since urged my own children to make the most of their celebration. Enjoy it to the max for you will never get that same opportunity again. Wear your gown as you drive away; open your own gifts; dance, laugh, and enjoy your party, this is the first day of the rest of your lives.

In the 50's it was customary for the bride to change from her wedding gown into a going away outfit. I made my appearance to my husband and the world, in a lovely blue suit embellished with sequins and embroidery, red high heels with sling backs, a matching bag and white gloves and hat; presenting myself as a married woman, eager to face her new world. The dress, shoes, purse and hat seemed to make that official.

I always pictured our final send off as a newly married couple, driving away with graffiti, tin cans and streamers bouncing and flying in the air. However, Will wanted no one to touch his new wax job. Ray escorted us in his car to a secluded place where he had it hidden.

We were making the escape into our own new world. Completely engaged in each other. I was sitting as close to Will as I could. When we reached the city limits, we noticed a flashing red light behind us. We were pulled over to a stop.

When the police officer asked Will if he was aware that he had exceeded the speed limit, he took a good look at us; saw us all dressed up and the flowers we were wearing.

He grinned and said, " Well....., it looks like where you are going, you don't need a ticket."

I never knew for sure, but the officer let us off so easily, that I always suspected that we had been set up by my mischievous brothers. They never owned up to it, but I still think it was one final bit of their humor to send us on our way!

Newly Weds

From this moment on, Our Lives were Our Own......

We had only one destination that night; 'to get outa Dodge'. We drove to Wichita. It had never occurred to us to make a room reservation. As we entered the city, we drove around until we found a vacancy sign and stopped. It was dark by now, and that made it difficult to see the surroundings or the condition of the motel. It was nothing fancy but we gave no thought to that. I, for sure was not accustomed to a fancy place anyway. We were just a couple of kids in love. All we saw or cared about was each other.

The only thing we had eaten since early lunch was a few bites of cake and ice cream. Will was famished. After taking in our bags, we went to the nearby coffee shop for something to eat. Rarely before had Will and I eaten in a restaurant I didn't even know how or what to order. So this was still new to me. Will ordered ham and eggs, his all time favorite and I very shyly ordered a grilled cheese sandwich and tomato soup. He had been my husband for only 4 or 5 hours so I guess I felt I should be careful not to order something too extravagant.

Finished eating, Will ushered me into the privacy of our room. We turned toward each other, taking in the fact that now, at last, we were alone, we were married, and no more loneliness. After a few passionate kisses, I slipped into the bathroom to change into the beautiful night gown that my mother had been so shocked to see. It had a lace bodice and a full skirt, double layered with sheer pink and blue chiffon. (Not as *transparent* as she thought.) As I looked into the mirror, I couldn't keep from giggling a bit at the thought of her reaction.

I slowly opened the door and came out to present myself to my new husband. We devoured each other with our eyes as we melted together in each others arms. We were free now, to unleash our passion. For so long, we had dreamed and fantasized of this moment. Never again, would we have to be apart. Here, we began to make our dreams come true. Reality replaced fantasies, making precious memories of discovering our love together, so new and unexplored, to store in your hearts for a lifetime.

Truly, I had chosen the worlds' kindest, most gentle man. My Prince Charming, who passionately loved me and would care for me as I'd always dreamed.

Will and I had chosen to wait until our wedding night to release our passion completely to each other. First, we were taught this was not only God's plan for his people, but it was part of His design. He knew life struggles and we would need to have a strong bond of commitment to each other to see it through. We had built our relationship on trust for each other. We knew and understood the measure of our passion over the past three years of sharing our love and desires. Even though our communication was mostly through our daily letters to each other, with only a few occasional visits, we had established a strong foundation for our love. This had already seen us through a few tests. We were ready.

◆

We returned to my parents home the 'morning after' to gather our things. My mother could not resist pulling me aside. With questioning eyes, and a low inquisitive voice she asked.

"Are you ok?" "I expect ……" , hesitating, not sure how to finish the sentence.

'Yes, Mother', I said, with a slight tone of dismissal, "I'm fine". It was not mentioned again.

Mother had very rarely spoken of the intimate part of marriage. She couldn't. If anything, it was only spoken in 'hush hush' tones as something to endure, never tenderly, never in detail of course. Her upbringing dated to the late 1800 and early 1900's and her views of men and marriage were somewhat antiquated.

Our Honeymoon

Wedding gifts and all my earthly belongings were packed into the car. We were ready to leave for our new home in Waukegan, Illinois.

I was leaving behind my childhood home, my parents, everything I had for so long held dear. In spite of our eagerness to enter this new life we had prepared for together, the parting was difficult. My parents had showered their love on me in the best way they could. They had provided well for me. They had instilled their values in me, some that I rejected, finding them old fashioned. Some that were engraved in my heart for the rest of my life and others that I would pick up later in life and pass on to the next generations.

Suddenly, my teen rebellion flashed before me. Why had I fought so hard for my independence? I felt now, as if I'd kicked and screamed my way through adolescents. A huge wave of regret combined with love came over me for the two people who had given me life, raised me, struggled with me, and loved me through my own struggles.

It grieved me to see their tears as we slowly drove away. Now as they stood there, the two of them, waving tearfully as I looked back, waving and blowing kisses out the window, they seemed old to me…..so fragile. Perhaps this was the first time I felt the vulnerability of time and distance, but only years later, could I really understand the void of having a child leave home for the last time.

At last, we were on our way. Just the two of us. Ready to begin our life together as we headed for North Chicago where Will had been working with the Veteran's Administration for the past two years.

❧

We traveled roads I'd never been before. Our whole life stretched out before us. With eagerness and the gentleness of a Prince, Will lead me forward.

With new eyes I eagerly took in the sights, as we traveled through unfamiliar country sides. The sense of adventure building anticipation in my young heart.

For miles before we crossed the state line between Kansas and Missouri, we had been seeing large billboards advertising the beautiful Lake of the Ozarks and all it's attractions. "Scenic Air Tours! Rides Given Every Hour" , "Take our Tom Sawyer Sight Seeing Cruiser around the Lake", or " Get 'Old Time' Photos Made Here"! We'd spent nearly every bit of our money for the wedding and for travel to our new home, so we passed up those tempting invitations. But when we saw a sign that read, "Visit the Amazing Bridal Caves, Next Right", it seemed appropriate that we should see it. It *was* our honeymoon after all, and I convinced Will to stop.

This was the first time I'd ever entered a cave. We were lead downward on a steep narrow path. While the temperature dropped with each descending step we were glad we had brought our light jackets.

Suddenly, we found ourselves in a very large room. A room of giant multicolored crystal columns, delicate icicles and massive ice draperies that took my breath away. Such beauty! Our eyes took it all in as we went through room after room, filled from floor to ceiling with incredible mineral deposits, each one different from the others. We were told that legendary Indian weddings were held down here a century earlier and one can still reserve the great room for a wedding ceremony. What amazing beauty lay under the earths surface. Truly a fantasy to behold.

Evening was upon us, so we found a motel where we could spent the night. Before we settled in, Will asked me if I wanted something more to eat. I said 'no' as we had eaten somewhat earlier. But, when we were snuggled down in bed, I felt the stirring of hunger in my stomach and I shyly mentioned it. For the first time I discovered that my timing was *not* good! Will was a kind and generous man, but the way he threw the covers back, pulled on his pants and asked what I wanted to eat held a distinct touch of resentment. Suddenly, I felt very foolish when I sensed that he was just a wee bit miffed about going out *just then*! When he returned and crawled back into bed, I couldn't help feeling the icicle between us. When I asked about it, he reminded me that he *had* asked earlier if I wanted anything. I realized then that he'd had other things in mind than going out looking for food. This was our first little tiff, and I remember being quite repentant, but it took a while for the tension to melt away.

Our First Home

The next day we drove through Illinois. The closer we got to Waukegan our anticipation rose to new heights.

Just weeks before our wedding, Will found a little cottage for us to live. Although he had described it to me in letters, he couldn't wait for me to see it.

Butterflies fluttered in my stomach and Will's eagerness was clear to me as he pointed out landmarks that guided us 'home'. It was evening when the car pulled to a stop. Will put his arm around me, pulled me close, kissed me and said, " This is it. Welcome home, darling." Then he got out of the car and came around to open my door and eagerly lead me inside. Giving me the grand tour of each square foot of our 3 room, 1 bath home. He eagerly hoped I would like it. Like it? I loved it!

He had described it very well in his letters and had fantasized of bringing me here. Finally, it had become reality. Here in this cozy little white cottage on the edge of town, we would begin our life. Just the two of us.

There were people who had anticipated our home coming. The Harvey's, our landlords, who lived just across the drive way, had freshened the house for us. They were an older couple who took us under their wings like a mother hen. It was an unequivocal love they showed us from the start. We began looking to them like family.

Our little home was completely furnished. Nothing fancy but adequate. We even had a TV! A large box with a 8 or 9 inch oval screen. I'd only seen one or two shows at a friends house before. This black and white screen in our living room opened a whole new world to me. Will and I spent many evenings enjoying drama and music. It also served as a textbook by observation for me on fashion, home decor or in social behavior.

Will's friends had paid a pre-homecoming visit and left our bed short sheeted and sprinkled heavily with rice. There was rice in the bathtub, rice in the TV, rice in every imaginable place they could find. In those days, it was customary for close friends….and maybe not so close friends, to give the newly married couple a 'chiveree.' This began as a gracious invitation to the couple for a party with friends, and to receive gifts. What the 'unaware' couple was not supposed to suspect, tricks could possibly be played on them.

I'd heard the story about one where the groom had to push his bride down the middle of main street in a wheel barrow. Some tricks were even cruel. We felt very fortunate just to have been showered with rice.

There were many discoveries to make. The neighborhood where we lived, the hospital where Will worked, new things about each other, driving through the countryside, were now going to be part of my life. We spent untold hours at the beach across town, basking in the sun and playing in the surf of Lake Michigan. Getting all dressed up and eating dinner in fine restaurants every Sunday after church, or in between, was a new discovery for me as well as going to movies. These had never been a part of my life before now. Movies were condemned by my parents and restaurants were an unnecessary expense. These discoveries quickly became our way of living that we pursued throughout our life together.

The hardest part of our honeymoon was the day Will had to return to work. Neither of us wanted to pull ourselves apart. Yet, I remember that first day, alone at home, enraptured in the fact that this was for real. I was now a housewife, and I filled the pleasant hours in my bright little kitchen, loading the white cabinets with clean new wedding dishes. The counter tops were bright red, the white appliances were older but nice. The table and chairs were my favorite. The table was a white enamel with red and chrome trim and the chairs matched. I eagerly made everything lovely for the moment my husband walked in the door at the end of the day.

In the days to follow, I tried out different task schedules, learning, for instance, there was neither time or necessity to scrub the bathroom with bleach from top to bottom every day. We didn't have a bathroom in the home where I grew up; only a path to the ugly, smelly old outhouse, so this was a special novelty for me. I was exploring the chores of a homemaker, joyfully learning as I went. When Will arrived home, we would have a nice dinner together. Admittedly, some of them didn't turn out as good as others, but he was gracious and never complained. Most of the time he would help with cleanup and he enjoyed fixing breakfast in the mornings.

Once I decided to make what his mother said was his most favorite dish. I painstakingly cooked the beans and added the pork and gravy, just as the recipe directed. It had turned out very well and I was so proud to serve it to him…… but he, somewhat doubtfully said it was 'pretty good'……

not wonderful as I'd expected. On questioning him further, he said, "Well, you didn't use Navy beans." I was shocked, disappointed, and taken aback. They were white beans. What difference did it make what name they were called? A bean was a bean, after all, in my opinion. I'd worked all day on this dish to make it perfect…and it *was* delicious…. but I failed. I was heartbroken . I discovered that I had a lot to learn. As long as I could follow a detailed recipe, I did pretty well. I don't recall Will ever making a negative comment on my cooking after that. In fact, through the years, he rarely failed to thank me or compliment me for the meals I prepared.

Misgivings in the Midst of Bliss

Since going into the 1-W service, Will had been working as an orderly in the Veteran's hospital and had been upgraded to a surgical technician, a role he found both inspiring and enjoyable. Our first week in Waukegan, he proudly took me to his work place and introduced me to his co-workers, nurses and other staff.

Everyone there was very gracious to me, but, I soon felt thrown into an environment where I was completely out of the loop. Will was at ease with those whom he had already built a rapport. I suddenly felt like that little tag-along girl of long ago, who was lost, wide-eyed, who didn't understand the 'language' and wanted her 'mommie'. I found their jokes and subject matter to contain a lot of erotic innuendos. I was not accustomed to the medical terms and the way they were flippantly used in a joking manner. This intensified my discomfort.

I had become quite accustomed to 'shady' jokes among my girl friends and I had even become at ease sharing them with Will. But this was different. This was men and women enjoying this type of banter together without reserve. I did not like him laughing at their jokes. I didn't trust them. To me it seemed flirtatious and I felt threatened. Even though Will tried to make me a part of it, I felt all alone, betrayed. I just wanted to curl up and cry. I was clearly out of my element.

The work relationships within that surgical unit seemed far too intimate for my comfort, thus began my life long struggle with women's flirtations with my husband. Compared to those silly girls that threw themselves at Will in high school, these women, older, more world-wise, seemed far more familiar with him now, and made me very uneasy.

Will was proud to have me by his side. He was always ready to assure me of his constant love and faithfulness. He was so attentive, always keeping my hand in his, or his arm protectively around me, but I believe my own insecurities prevented me from seeing the devotion and commitment Will had for me, causing me to fall into an escalade of fear.

Walking into his world, the world outside my comfort zone, was very difficult for me. I had begun to deeply resent the nurses that he worked with every day. Feelings of jealousy began eating at my mind. I'd formed the opinion that they thought I was too naïve and felt sorry for Will. This lead me to question the motives of any woman who seemed overly friendly with Will and remained a problem for me for many years to come. We both began to realize how unsure I was of myself. Thankfully, Will loved me so much, that he made it his life goal to gently but surely build my trust on every new level we encountered.

When I say 'life goal', I mean just that. I had a lot of growing up to do, a lot of learning about life, but so did he. We were so very young. But we worked at it together. Through mountains of fears and rivers of tears, our love and commitment always brought us through life's deepest waters, only to bind us closer.

I wanted to be a part of all his world and he was eager to include me. Occasionally when he was called away from home in an evening or a weekend, he would take me with him. Although I was not allowed into the operating room itself, I was allowed to watch through a window. I observed with great interest the hurried, masked surgical staff, surrounded by bright lights, sheets, stainless steel buckets and pans, and....blood. Always blood, as they focused intently on their job of saving a life. Will was one of them, working to save someone's life and I felt such a welling up of pride. Although, I could not see the actual intricate work from that distance, I became more and more interested to know what he saw.

He had asked to watch an autopsy. He told me later that it left a deep impression upon him that he kept picturing long after the event. However, this was a story he loved to tell over and over in years to come when the autopsy was complete, the doctor placed a tag on the cadaver's big toe which read, "Good Housekeeping Seal of Approval." The doctor further explained to Will that occasionally other doctors questioned the quality of his work, so this little tag was his final insurance.

Learning New Things

Will loved his work at the hospital. He even thought of going to school to become a nurse. Male nurses were not as socially recognized in those days as they are now, yet the idea played on his mind. The suggestion of his going back to school was frightening for me. I'm sure it was the thought of his working in that environment that made me so uncomfortable and frightened me. If only I could have been mature enough then to recognize his potential and encourage him. There turned out to be other interests that he would consider in years to come. In time, as we dealt with these 'threats' to my security by women who worked with Will, he admitted to me that this kind of interplay did give opening to thoughts of infidelity. Over a long process, we both learned more about trust and how to avoid these situations.

I took a job in the dietician's office at the Vet's hospital, typing weekly menus and answering phones from the wards when diets were changed for certain patients. There were no computers then, no copy machines. So every sheet of paper in the typewriter had to have carbons layered between paper to duplicate the information. Typing errors in that situation were not easily repaired. I tried to keep up, but I couldn't work as fast as they needed. So 6 months later I took a job as a clerk at the Globe Department Store in downtown Waukegan. I was assigned to the Sewing Notions department.

My mother had always sewn my clothes when I was growing up. I took a sewing class in high school, and now all the pretty fabrics and exciting sewing tools available peaked my interest. I shared my discoveries with Will, realizing I would like to try my hand at sewing, He began quietly doing some research, and to my surprise he gave me a new sewing machine. It was so exciting for me to actually buy some of those items I'd been selling to my customers. Will decided he would like to learn too. He picked out some fabric and a pattern for a pair of pajamas. I was supposed to teach him, but teaching him to sew was like putting a bull in the drivers seat with a heavy hoof on the pedal! Fabric flew, threads clogged up and when my patience wore thin, I quickly realized this was not a challenge I was prepared for....nor was he. I think we both bagged that project and sent it to the waste basket.

Will continually introduced me to many wonderful things that I had never experienced before. He took me to my first movie. Movies had been strictly banned in my Christian circle. I was led to believe that God would strike me dead if I went somewhere that 'God would not go'. Yet, I could not understand why. After a few movies I lost my fear, realizing I had *not* been struck dead. I became hooked on movies from the start. Later, I was to learn that God *is* everywhere; he doesn't draw the line at the door of a movie theater.

This was only one of many things that I'd been restricted from doing as I was growing up. Wearing make up, wearing shorts or a bathing suit were only a few on the long list. My mother came by train to visit for a couple of weeks. When we went to pick her up at the station in Chicago, the first thing she noticed was that I was wearing lipstick.

It was very hard for her to adjust to that and I had to listen to a few lectures on falling into *sin*, but was not to be intimidated. I could decide these things for myself now. It took me many years to realize that God looks at our heart rather than the outward person.

Our first guests, were friends of Will's visiting from Idaho. We wanted to treat them with a special dinner. Not knowing that certain cuts of meat were more tender than others, we bought a round steak. Our guests graciously fought their way through its toughness while we tried to hide our embarrassment, but years later we all would laugh about it.

Going to different restaurants trying different foods, was such a delight. We were eating Chinese food, Italian food, Mexican food; having all sorts of food adventures, many times sharing meals with other friends.

There were always new places to go. Nearly every weekend we had experiences that I had never had before. One weekend we planned to go to the Wisconsin State fare in Milwaukee. Before we went, Will took me to get a new outfit that became my favorite of all time! It was a denim two piece skirt and top in a western style and a western hat to wear. I felt like a rodeo queen! To a young girl from a little farm in Kansas, I couldn't get enough of this new life.

Will took me to the department store to buy my first bathing suit. The thought of appearing in public so scantily dressed...The very idea! *'Oh, if mama could see me now'*, I thought as I tried on the suit and modeled it for him. But he liked what he saw and bought it for me.

Lake Michigan was right across town from where we lived. I had never been swimming and didn't know how to swim. Frankly, I was afraid of the water, but Will quickly taught me how to play in the water and still keep my head above it. We couldn't wait for each evening to get home from work and head for the beach. Many times we built a fire and roasted hot dogs and marshmallows. Then we would spread a blanket and lay there listening to the crashing of the waves until dark.

The two major museums in Chicago, the Fields Museum of Natural History and the Museum of Science and Industry were amazing places to visit. Show case after show case of historical events depicted there, far beyond our comprehension. One could not see it all in one day. We went as often as we could, but you could go there for a life time and still find more. We also learned about star patterns and how the planets lined up in the universe at the Adler Planetarium. So much to do, so much to see. we never saw it all.

Fall came with the change of season. While the weather was still warm, we took a drive along the lake to the Wisconsin Dells. We rented a boat to go out on the water. We were taken in by the beautiful scenery and enjoying the view until a large tourist boat came by and sent a huge wake our way. Will turned the boat into the wake, hoping we would ride over it, but the motor was not powerful enough and the wave washed over us. We were not prepared for that and suddenly it felt as if we were fighting for our lives. I became terrified and quite certain we were both going to drown. While I shrank to the bottom of the boat, whimpering and holding on for dear life, Will calmly kept control of the inadequate boat and steered it safely back to shore. Like a couple of drowned rats, scared and wet, we headed back to our hotel room to get dry and snuggle under warm covers.

First Christmas and a New Year

Choosing a tree from a lot down town for our first Christmas was such fun. It was so large, we barely got it inside the house. We actually had to watch our tiny TV between branches. It took up most of our small living room that held a large oil burning heating stove, the TV and a couch. If we could have gotten it in, I'm sure we would have had a larger one still. This was our first Christmas together and what a celebration that was! Buying our first tree, first lights; decorations and shopping for gifts for each other and to send home, all were so exciting. When all the other lights were turned off, I would sit with Will's arms around me on the sofa watching the beautiful lights twinkle on and off, as we took in the magic of the moment.

Hours were spent watching variety shows with dramatized stories on Ford Theater, The General Electric Hour, Fireside Theater or watching the Hit Parade on our little TV were favorites. There were others too, but non as wonderful as Red Skelton or Red Buttons, Jack Benny or Lucy.

The winter air had a crispness to it as it blew off of Lake Michigan that bordered the city of Waukegan. The streets were covered with glistening snow. When daylight faded away, the street lights came on, giving everything a golden glow. Street lights and store fronts were decorated and lit up in bright colors. You could hear the jingle of Salvation Army bell ringers at every corner. In the distance, the sound of carols could be heard over loud speakers. I will never forget making our way from store to store, the magical sights of that Christmas. The sounds of fresh snow crunch under our feet as we strolled amid the silent wet snow flakes felling on our faces. Somehow, it felt like I was watching myself from a distance, like a fantasy; in love and on the arm of my handsome lover. The world, my world was at peace.

I knew exactly what I would buy for Will. For months now, he had been slouching around in those awful clods he called slippers. Actually they were old canvas shoes he had cut the back out,... slouchy and tattered. As I look back now, I see that even then he was frugal enough to put aside his own need in order to save money for us to get married. But, I didn't understand that then. I went shopping in a real 'gentleman's store' and found some nice leather gentleman slipper, which I proudly carried home and put under the tree.

While I was shopping for his Christmas gift, Will got the urge to take a look at new cars. A brand new 1956 black Ford Fairlane caught his eye and wouldn't let him go. When we met up again, he eagerly steered me to the dealers showcase where stood the object of his dreams. Oh, it was lovely! Shinny black with chrome trim, the interior was white with leather seats. A real beauty... besides it smelled so good. It didn't take much for him to convince me to buy it. What fun we had driving around in that car, feeling like a million bucks! Looking back, we have to wonder how we could afford a new car when our rent was $75 and Will brought home little more than $50 a week. My small salary certainly didn't amount to much, but we managed to eat out a lot and go to movies all the time. $2100 for a new car that would last indefinitely, *perhaps the rest of our lives*, was certainly a 'good investment' in our estimation.

Speaking of investments, we decided if we got a different apartment, we could invest our money in new furniture. We discussed this idea with our dear landlords. By now they were playing a strong paternal role in our life. They convinced us that was *not* a good investment so we stayed in our little furnished cottage.

On Christmas afternoon, Jerry and another friend, Vernon, came to play some games. Later, dressed in our best, we went together to a prestigious restaurant in Gurnee, Illinois, called the *Rustic Manor*. The Manor was a lovely log ranch style, with log interior décor. Soft music and low lighting set the stage for an evening of elegant dining while male waiters served delicious entrées or brought special drinks ordered from the bar.

On occasion, Jerry brought some beer or other drinks to our house, but I had never had a cocktail before. I had my first "pink lady." It was so tangy and delicious! But since the drinks cost two dollars each, I only had one.

We looked over the menu and the specialty of the house was their "Steak and Lobster for $4.95 a plate," however, since we didn't have a lot of money, we chose something less expensive.

Later, at home, Will opened a bottle of champagne. The cork popped and shot across the room, a shout of glee arose as most of it sprayed all over the walls and ceiling. A lovely merry first Christmas!

Shopping at Marshal Fields

We often took trips into Chicago to visit the wonderful museums, or have dinner and a movie. We even took an evening cruise on the lake to see the beautiful lights on shore; visited a radio station where they were airing a weekly drama, played by a friend Will had met while working at the Seminary.

We had been married just 12 months when we visited The Fair and Marshall Fields, both prestigious department stores in the heart of Chicago called 'The Loop'. Now, over 50 years later, they no longer exist. One visit to Marshall Fields stands out among the others.

Will has always loved books and read a lot, so he was drawn to the book department in Marshall Fields. I wandered off to look at other books that interested me. Suddenly, I had a strange buzzing in my head and darkness clouded my eyes ….

Faintly, I heard someone say, "Oh, the poor girl, I wonder what happened? Does anyone know who she is? "

As I began to open my eyes, I was lying on the floor with a sea of faces peering down at me asking me questions.

Immediately I felt embarrassed for creating a scene and I asked for my husband, who was promptly by my side. After taking a little time to recover, he escorted me out of the building to the car.

There was a police officer by our car, writing up a ticket because we had exceeded time on the parking meter. Will explained to him what had happened, but he didn't seem to care...until Will reached into his pocket and pulled out his hand clutching a couple of bills and held them tightly in his fist as he handed it to the officer. After cautiously looking around, the officer took the bills, put away his ticket pad and wished us a 'good day'. I'm sure the officer expected more than the $2 he received, but by then we were driving down the street.

A day or two later, we saw a doctor , who confirmed that I was pregnant. Pregnant! We were going to have a baby! We were so excited that we had actually made a baby! The idea was so new. The realization had to work into our minds slowly. The due date, January of 1957 , seemed like such a long time away. We couldn't wait to spread the news.

I couldn't wait to begin wearing maternity clothes, even though it would be weeks before I would even begin to get a baby belly. I bought a pattern and some fabrics to make some tops. They were designed like a tent big enough to cover a pregnant elephant! Fashionable though, just like every expectant mother wore. The idea, I think, was to hide the suggestion that a baby was somewhere under there and how it may have gotten there. In the 50's, folks began to be more open about speaking of pregnancy without embarrassment. Still in some circles, you might have heard someone say in hushed tones and a serious look, that I was "in the family way."

Very soon though, I had to stop working at the store because I had developed a mild complication and the doctor ordered me to bed for a couple of weeks. Thankfully, all was well and my pregnancy progressed without further incident.

Will's Encounter with Fate

Will had given up his job at the Veteran's Hospital and was now working for a loan company. One dark night, he quickly learned that loan companies in the Chicago area were different from the ones back home. It was his job to track down clients, who habitually avoided making their payments.

By making surprise visits to their homes, he might catch them unaware and talk to them. Often he would find no one at home so he would sit in his car in the dark and wait, more often than not without success. These seemed to be a game of cat and mouse that was played among the clients and the lenders.

On one cold winter night he went to a small neighboring town to make a collection. Will parked his car down the street from the house and waited. Finally he gave up on the client and started driving home when he sensed he was being followed. The car behind kept up with him on a stretch of dark road. When he sped up, the car behind sped up as well. At the point of top speed the car behind came up along side, parallel to Will. At this neck breaking speed the car door opened and a man stood with his gun pointed directly at Will's head.

An inexplicable fear gripped him. Will tried to speed up, but they were right with him, the gun aimed at his head. Fearing for his life, on this dark winter night, sweat poured from his pores as his white slippery hands gripped the steering wheel, trying to maintain control of his car. Mile after mile these two cars dodged each other, back and forth as they sped through the darkness until the lights of the Waukegan city limits came into view. The gunman retreated back inside the car, but the gun remained clearly visible. Still pointing at his head. Still racing through town, Will hoped beyond hope a police officer would intervene, but there were non in sight. His only other recourse was to head straight for the Police station but before he reached his destination, the other car fled a different direction. In front of the station, Will ran in to report the car and give the license number, but the car was not to be found. We learned later that police often had an *understanding* with people like that, so any report would be ignored .

Once at home, that near fateful night, Will stumbled into the house. As always, so glad he was home I rushed to meet him, when suddenly I noticed his chalk white face, his trembling body and his damp wool suit soaked with sweat, reeking with the smell of fear. First checking the lock on the door, he turned to grabbed me and held on tightly I could feel him trembling against me, his breath still coming quickly, until he could regain composure enough to tell me of his close brush with death.

A few days later, on his way into Chicago, following the flow of traffic, he saw this same client ahead of him. He followed for a distance hoping he would signal him to a stop. Instead the client sped up, weaving in and out of heavy traffic with Will behind him. Will turned into the oncoming lane trying to pull along side him. But they kept driving. Suddenly he looked up to see a semi truck coming full speed at him. He knew he needed to squeeze back into his own lane before he got hit. But the client refused to let him in. As the massive truck bore down on him it let out a loud warning blast with his horn. But there was no break in the traffic. Will knew this would probably be the end......

But just at the last possible moment the client slowed and let him in, avoiding the truck. The client pulled to the side of the road and stopped. Trembling from the close call, Will was sure that the man would likely blow him away and braced himself.

Instead, the client thundered at him, "What do you think you're doing? Trying to get us both killed?" But it turned out to be quite an amiable encounter with a promise to make a payment and both going their own separate ways.

We learned that bookies used loan companies to fund their gambling habits. This was all big business connected with the Mafia.

This experience sharpened Will's sense of self-preservation and security not only for himself and for his family, but also for anyone else around him. He had always had a keen interest in weapons, but now this interest became more than a personal passion. The security of his family was foremost on his mind for the rest of his life.

These experiences colored his life in so many different ways. He was the protector. He was the one who always made sure our seat belts were buckled. He was the 'door keeper' who never failed to check the locks. We always knew we were safe when he was in charge.

Will soon quit that job and tried a few others. He sold vacuum cleaners for a day, he took care of the grounds at

Mundelein Catholic Seminary, and worked for a contractor that paid him with a rubber check.

Then he landed a job as a cook at our favorite restaurant, the *Rustic Manor*, where we'd had dinner on special occasions during the past year.

Working nights and coming home from the restaurant smelling like a cooked lobster wasn't how Will saw his life in a few years. His father had been asking him for help on the farm. In his mind, the free life of the farm, and the open spaces were calling.   Soon we packed up our things, said goodbye to our wonderful life of new discoveries in Waukegan and moved to Idaho.

Our honeymoon cottage faded in the rear view mirror as we left Waukegan, knowing we would never again return to those magical days. Both of us were silently thinking our own thoughts, treasuring the discoveries we had made together, grieving the loss of our solitude. Now, we traveled the long road ahead to new adventures.

What Lies Ahead

My brief visit to Idaho, three years earlier, left me with the cherished memories of being together all day every day among the pristine images of beautiful mountains and the blue-gray sagebrush where Will loved to hunt for jackrabbits.

For the past year and a half, we'd had no one to look over our shoulder, no critical eye looking at us as we worked our way into a marriage relationship. We answered to no one except each other. The difference now was that we would temporarily share a home with his parents until we found a place of our own. Surely, for us now, giving up that private paradise was the hardest part of all.

Midway on our journey across country, we stopped in Kansas, to visit with my family. Once back in my childhood home it seemed that the maturity that I'd gained over the past months of marriage quickly regressed. Although my father didn't seem to have trouble adjusting to my new role, I became a little girl again in my mother's eyes and some of my old resentments resurfaced. I often found myself snapping at her comments in defense of how I dressed or thought. She worried that my spirituality was jeopardized by my marriage and my soul was lost for eternity. She even told me she would rather I'd died as an infant than be married to Will. She had lost control over me and didn't know how to deal with it. This caused her to say hurtful things she didn't really mean. Her difficulty in letting me be myself created stress for all of us. It was time to move on.

We arrived in Idaho where we were welcomed by Will's parents. They were particularly pleased to see that I was already showing signs of a new grandchild for them.

Will was eager to get back to walking the fields with his irrigation shovel, a pleasant task that he had enjoyed in his earlier days at home. He had looked forward to working the soil in Idaho and to building a life and a home for his family. His dream to carry on the family farm when his father retired, invigorated him.

Most of the summer crops were harvested, fields tilled and the winter wheat planted. Soon it would be time for the fall potatoes and sugar beets to be dug. The harvest consisted of long days, hard work of running machines, trucking the crops to individual cellars or to town, loading and unloading, and coming in late every evening, worn out, covered with dust, ready for a hot meal and a comfortable bed. After the harvest was finished, came the reward of a job completed, some free time and payment for the crops. Being part of the harvest team was a way of earning a nice chunk of change for the season. Schools are let out, women and men took the job of driving potato and beet trucks through out the harvest. When one farmers field was finished, they in turn joined the next farmers team, keeping the process moving until all the fields were empty. Will looked forward to this.

It quickly became apparent that what Will really was needed at home for, was to be a pipe mover. Willie Harder had nearly two thousand acres in the desert several miles west of Aberdeen, some of which was planted into winter wheat and needed to be sprinkler irrigated. This method of irrigation was done by running 40 ft long sections of heavy pipe along the ground at various increments and they needed to be carried by hand to the next location to water the whole field.

After a long lonely day of kluging over rough wet terrain in knee-high rubber boots and carrying these pipes for a full day, Will would drag home just in time for a late supper. After soaking his aching muscles in a hot tub of water and breaking away from Father's lengthy oration of the events of *his* own day, Will could finally join me in our room where he would fall into bed. I made a nightly ritual of massaging his weary bones until he fell asleep exhausted in my arms.

I became very lonely for my husband throughout those long days he was away in the field and when he came home, I had to share him with his parents. Will's mother, tidy and organized, treated me graciously as she would a guest, but there it seemed to stop. If I offered a hand at anything, she preferred to do it herself. There was very little to talk about with her and it felt very awkward. Time grew very heavy on my hands. After a short time of doing nothing but take lots of naps, I went into town and picked out some fabrics and patterns, unpacked my sewing machine and went to work sewing things for myself and our expected baby. It was enough to fill my day, but there always seemed a chill in the atmosphere until Will came home.

Will and I agreed taking our new car out to the desert on the unpaved and rough roads would not be good. Idaho dust is very fine and filters into every possible crevice so occasionally, I was allowed to use his parents car to take Will some lunch.

A few times they announced they were taking *our* car somewhere. They didn't request the use of our new car, they just told us. On one such occasion, I fixed Will a lunch and drove their older car out to the desert where he worked. They were not expected back until quite late, so the rest of the day, I played house and prepared a wonderful meal for just the two of us. But just at the time Will arrived his parents drove in….hungry. My balloon was burst. I had only enough food for two. Mom shooed me out of the kitchen and took over, while I disappeared into the bedroom for a good cry.

Work shut down for Sunday as that was the day of rest. Early on those mornings Will and I would get up and try to leave the house before we could be coerced into going to church or some social event that his mother cooked up in our behalf. We looked forward to those days with great eagerness.

We would grab a hamburger and drive up into the mountains; or venture into Pocatello to eat and go to a movie. Sometimes we went to the airport where Will loved to sit and watch the airplanes. Occasionally we would just go sit by the lake. Every moment we could be alone together was cherished.

Will was not getting paid as promised and we had a baby coming, a new car to pay for, and we longed for a place of our own. His father gave a little money now and then, which seemed more like a pittance that was just enough to keep us dependant on him. There were no jobs available aside from a low-paid farm hand, which he already was. Every rental we looked at was too expensive, so he began writing letters to various Veterans' hospitals around the Northwest, looking for work. We were excited to receive a letter of acceptance from the hospital in Palo Alto, California.

Will's Childhood

It's hard to describe, why I could not feel quite 'at home' with Will's family. They seemed so different from him. I often wondered how it was possible that he was from a family who seemed to lack emotion and warmth and greeted each other with hand shakes rather than a hug or bursts of joy, It felt so cold to me.

Will was not like that. I can only imagine what a tender little boy Will was by just looking at the pictures and hearing his stories of when he was small.

He was the youngest of 5. Born on a farm in Kansas and later moved with his family to Idaho when he was just 7 years old. I was always fascinated by the story of that trip.

In 1940 the entire family crowded into a 1937 automobile. Mom, dad, 2 sisters, an older brother and grandma with little Wilfred sitting on a organ stool between the front and back seat. The oldest sister had already left home for nursing school. When he got too tired, he could stretch out across the laps in the back seat and take a nap. It took several days of travel to Idaho on two lane roads, not always paved.

Knowing his mother, I'm quite sure they had brought plenty of food along to last the long trip.

All the household goods had been shipped from Kansas by rail, including the used lumber from their old torn down homestead at Brainerd, Kansas. A few days prior to their arrival in Idaho, the goods were unloaded on a railroad siding called "Strang's Station" adjoining the property of their new home. By the time the family arrived, relatives had already moved the items into the house and barn where they were to live.

The house was a small two story rock structure, built around 1906. It had originally been designated for a cheese house with 12 inch cement walls to keep it cool in the summer. It was used for a dwelling instead. Two rooms were at ground level with one big room upstairs, the only access being an outside stairway. For a time, the family made do by using one downstairs room as a bedroom for Mom, Dad and Grandma while the other was used for all other purposes such as living, cooking, and family dining.

Wilfred, only seven years old, and his two older sisters had to go out in the winter snow and climb the stairs at bedtime. They had no extra heat. They would tuck hot water bottles or bricks that had been warmed in the oven under the heavy comforters at the foot of the bed to keep them warm. In the morning it was a mad rush, with teeth chattering, running again down the outside stairs and inside to warm themselves. Backing up to a glowing 'pot belly' wood stove, they would often end up with a nice brand, by getting their behind too close.

There were many areas on this new place for a small boy to explore. The orchard provided places to play and hide. The irrigation ditches and wildlife surrounding the farm held many more fascinations. Other than a few cousins who came to visit now and then, he was quite alone. Mom and sisters were busy with house and garden and his father was too busy with his farm to spend any time with him.

His brother, 11 years older, played pranks on him, taunted him by telling scary stories that gave him nightmares, or peeking through the bathroom window and poking fun to embarrass him. Beyond that, he showed little interest in him. Between the big brother's scary stories and his big sister's obsession with the devil, his dreams took on many frightening forms.

One particular incident that stayed fresh in Will's mind his whole life long, was waking up to a frightful roaring sound and a whirlwind that caught him up, spun him around over head before throwing him back on his bed. This frightened him beyond reason. As with all the nightmares, he left his bed in fear and ran to his sisters bed. Everyone believed this to be another one of his terrifying dreams, but he always remembered himself to be awake. This was not a dream. No one ever convinced him otherwise. Seems, there was more emphasis placed on speaking about the devil and dodging demons than teaching him of God's love and care for His children, thus creating a lot of confusion in a little boy's mind.

He found pleasure in assisting his mother in household tasks. In years to come, whenever Will helped me in the kitchen he would say, " It was always special when I got to dry dishes for my mom."

In comparison to my own childhood, the nature of Will's family was far different from mine. My siblings and I openly showed our affection as well as opinions. My mom and dad regularly showed their love to us. On the other hand , they rarely showed affection to each other or found things they could agree on. I always knew that I was loved. Mom's lap was always available, even when we had outgrown it and I have memories of my father holding me too. Many times he sat by my bed, telling me story after fascinating story of his life growing up. How I loved those stories both of my parents told me of when they were young. I would beg for more and more.

In contrast, Will never remembered being told he was loved. I never could understand why the words "I love you" were never spoken in his home. He doesn't remember sitting on his mothers lap as a little child; being held or snuggled as a way of giving love or comfort.

He was taught the basics of religious beliefs and respect for others, but the expression of love and emotion seemed non-existent. The household was quiet and emotionally numb. In fact, his mother had taught him "never show your feelings." On hearing that, I became very angry. Of course! This answered many questions regarding the difficulty I had getting him to express some of his feelings about things! This gave me better understanding of the stoic environment in their home. Facing an issue openly, head on, simply wasn't done. Feelings and emotions were kept tightly hidden inside.

It was not his feelings of love for me that were hard for him to express. Those he did eloquently. But the feelings of rejection or his inner feelings regarding discord was very hard for him.

It was a life-long process for Will to learn to express his feelings openly. On the occasions when we were around his family, it was very easy for him to slip back into the silent mode. But, he worked very hard to overcome the need to withhold his emotions from me. Over the years he became a good communicator.

There was no real closeness with his father. Willie, as his father was called, was driven by the need to succeed in his work, which was farming. There was little time for Wilfred as a little boy, nor did Willie take time to play. His father bought him a rifle when he was 10 or so, but it was his mother who taught him how to shoot. I found out later, Willie was quite a conversationalist with his acquaintances. He had many friends. He never knew a stranger, and was always interested in people and their views. Yet, when it came to his family, they showed him little respect and his opinions were often devalued.

Around the age of 10, Wilfred found enjoyment in helping the carpenter who was building an addition to their home. They used the lumber brought from Kansas, giving the Idaho house a piece of additional history. Later, Wilfred attempted to build a tree house in the orchard. It was never finished, although some remnants still remain.

The teen years were difficult for Wilfred. He spent much of his time alone, reading in his room, or hunting rabbits when he wasn't in school. He helped with potato harvest and other farm related chores. But through the winter months when there was less to do. He isolated himself and became overweight. He was not a happy kid. Other than occasional visits with his cousins and church acquaintances, he became more and more secluded. Somehow he didn't feel like he fit in.

Many times, he was troubled with dark thoughts that encroached his mind. With no one to confide in, no one to help him through this, he struggled on his own. This left him in a state of confusion and a very lonely young man. Even then he began questioning his standing with God.

He didn't feel well much of the time; had developed lots of colds and missed a lot of school. He was allowed to take the bus to Lava Hot Springs and spend a week soaking in the hot pools. His parents thought this would help him. All this time alone resulted in more depression. A doctor finally discovered he had an abscessed tooth which could be causing the sinus problem. It was removed, after which he began to feel better. He set about to lose weight and recover but, by now he had missed most of his school year. Returning to school was difficult as he was now in classes behind his friends.

Word from Kansas relatives came that there was a Christian high school in their community. Perhaps this would be a new start for Wilfred. Plans were made to put him on a train and he was sent to Berean Academy at Elbing, Kansas to begin the second term of his junior year.

This opened a new door for him. He reconnected with some of his relatives, quickly made new friends and began a new phase of his life. Everyone perceived him as a happy-go-lucky guy. Here, people saw him as a person of notable quality, yet with a certain shyness about him too. They were drawn to him like a magnet. Who could have known about his lonely past?

California, Here we come!

In November of 1956, towing a U Haul trailer behind our '56 Ford Fairlane, with all our possessions and an expected baby tucked safely inside the 'oven', we set out for a new life in sunny California. My due date was just 5 weeks away. Will had created a soft 'bed' in the back seat of our car where I could curl up when I needed to rest.

With a meager few dollars in our pocket, some sandwiches his mother had made for us, a few jars of canned apples, we were merrily on our way. We were going to *California!* A paradise I'd imagined since I was a child. Kind of like the land of fairytales to me. I'd heard about how green, how warm, how beautiful it was and it felt like a dream was coming true. I could hardly wait to get there.

We began traveling west, on State Highway 30 that followed the Snake River This river began from a small stream in Wyoming and cut between high mountain ranges and valleys, flowing, winding westward through Idaho into Oregon and empties into the Columbia River. Lakes and reservoirs were built along the way, providing water sports, fishing and irrigation water for farmers such as Will's father.

Will was eager to show me the Hanson hanging bridge over the Snake River Canyon. The highest bridge of it's kind anywhere, located in the part of Idaho we would be driving through. For now, the river had disappeared in a different direction. Taking an exit from the highway onto a paved county road he drove for a distance that lead us past a few farms. I noticed that the road curved to the left, but he kept going straight which became more of a dusty trail than a road. I figured he knew where he was going….so I said nothing…. until, we found ourselves, pulling our trailer down a cow path through a little green pasture, dotted with sagebrush and rock, cow pies and surrounded by a herd of sheep.

The man leading his sheep stared at us most inquisitively. Embarrassed, Will gave the man a wave and gingerly proceeded on through his barnyard, past his house and on out to the road again, just as if he knew what he was doing. Perhaps that man is still scratching his head in wonder at that strange car with an Illinois license plate, pulling a U Haul trailer. Of course, by now, Will noticed that he must have missed the road he should have taken.

As we drove past rock and sagebrush, the Snake River Canyon seemed to appear out of no where. From a distance, one would not expect this enormous crevice in the earths surface. Stretching for miles, curving this way and that; it's depth was breathtaking. At the very bottom flowed the Snake River. For at one point the highway took us along side of the river and suddenly we were looking down on it, hundreds of feet below. All due to Shoshone Falls that spilled 212 feet over mammoth rock. They say these falls are higher than Niagara Falls.

Turning westward we left the Snake River and Idaho behind. We saw nothing for hundreds of miles but flat country with baron hills in the distance; occasional cattle grazing on dry grass. It seemed as if the Nevada desert would never end. By evening, we came to the small town of Lovelock where we got a motel room and dined on the sandwiches and fruit that Will's mother had sent along.

Continuing west, the next morning, we knew we were getting close to California when we began to see mountains. Ahead of us, out of the desert sagebrush arose the city of Reno. The terrain changed drastically as we traveled out of the city and the ribbon of highway began to wind around, and around the high Sierras with a new view beyond each curve.

Through stories I'd heard of California, my own mind had conjured up pictures of a perfect land filled with orange groves and green fields. For now, all we saw were cedars and pines with the Sierra mountains towering above them.

We laughed when my mother warned that we may not be allowed to cross the border. But, she was recalling when in the 1930's, people from the Midwest states streamed into California. Their lives had been nearly wiped out by devastating dust storms that took their homes, their crops, even entire families. Depression and death surrounded these people so when word had drifted eastward about a land of milk and honey, where water flowed and green grass grew, the brave gathered up what fragments they had left of their families and possessions. Their only means of transportation, an old truck or car loaded with everything they could pile or tie on and the few meager coins they could scrape together, headed west. California held the promise of a new life. It was the place to go. Migrants filled with new hope streamed across the desert to reach this Mecca, only to be turned away at the state line if they did not have the 50cents entry fee. That was another era and another 'world'. Still, having only a small amount of money on us and migrating into California with all our possessions; in a small way Will and I could relate to that time.

Butterflies fluttered in my stomach as a big sign that read, "Welcome to California" came into view. And yes, they did let us in, contrary to what my mother had warned. After all, this was now 1956. Her facts were caught in a time warp of nearly 30 years earlier.

All cars had to stop at the port of entry, to show any fruit that was being carried in. Since fruit is one of California's largest crops that feeds not only our country, but also the world, they could not risk disease or insects from outside the border that could possibly contaminate the fruit in this state. But as most cars, we were waved through..

By mid-day, we had driven out of the mountains. The valley spread before us as far as the eye could see in every direction, a beauty like I'd never seen before. It truly appeared to be the beautiful land of milk and honey as the interstate wove through lush farm land and crossed flowing rivers. Eventually we came to the inlet of San Francisco Bay that continued to swell the nearer it flowed toward the ocean. The smell of sea salt and fish in the pungent bay air waft into the car as we passed. The body of water grew wider, debris had washed up along the shoreline, the sights and sounds of the water splashing, the fog horns blowing, the busy coming and going of tug boats and cargo boats on the water were such a sight to behold. The Oakland Bay Bridge was the longest, highest bridge we had ever seen. Crossing over, the city of San Francisco set on hills, greeted us, with it's skyscrapers pointing heavenward. Just beyond them we caught a glimmer of the Pacific Ocean.

The roads and streets crisscrossed over and under each other like the tangled underbrush of a concrete jungle. Traffic was going in every direction. I had never seen such a maze. But following large overhead signs with arrows pointing us in the right direction, it got us through the city.

As we drove down the peninsula southward, we never really left the city, The San Francisco Bay was now on the left side as Interstate 5 moved closer, then farther, then closer again to the water. On either side, city after city melded together as one, until mid-afternoon when we arrived in the beautiful city of Palo Alto.

Palo Alto, California

Our destination reached; this would become our home for the next 20 years. We stopped at a gas station to fill our tank and pick up a newspaper and a city map. We found an affordable apartment to sublet right away. The lady was just moving out that weekend. After seeing us, so young and my huge baby belly, she was very trusting and let us pay her half down and the rest in a month after Will received his first pay check. She would be out by noon the next day and we could move right in. We felt so fortunate.

Our first little home in California was a small, cozy fully-furnished studio apartment. A little galley served as a kitchen. The rest was living area that converted to sleeping space at night. A bathroom was just off of the living area. Across the busy street was the railroad. Trains would stop and go at different intervals, bells clanging at the intersection and brakes screeching at all hours, day and night, letting off commuters that traveled from city to city.

Noisy as it was, it had it's own ambience that held a certain charm for me, reminding me that I was now in 'the city' and gave me a certain feeling of distinction. I remember lying in bed, the bright street lights shining through the curtains. Seeing the apartment in this light, listening to the train sounds outside, made everything feel like a fantasy to me. In retrospect there was nothing outstanding about this apartment, but I'd never had anything so nice before. And in just a few weeks this is where we would be bringing our new baby.

The early November days were balmy. There was much within the community to explore. While Will was at work at his new job at the hospital, I went for long walks. I breathed in deeply these warm days of California autumn, filled with the sights, sounds, and smells that seemed to enveloped it all into a gloriously mysterious package. The trees and grass were bright green with only a touch here and there of fall color, and nearly every yard had the lush blooms of chrysanthemums. There were sidewalks everywhere that led to parks and shopping centers.

Even my doctor was within walking distance. Very soon now, I would be having my baby. I had no idea what to expect. The doctor had asked me about anesthesia. I had no idea what that was. I told him I think I just wanted to have my baby naturally, thinking it would save us money. That was all he seemed interested in knowing. He never inquired to see if I knew what to expect. He just handed me a very old book on natural childbirth, similar to one my mother had hidden away. One, that I occasionally peeked at when she was out of the house. I accepted the book and went on my way.

Christmas was just days away. We had no money to spend. It had taken every dollar we had to secure the apartment and buy a little food. Since our baby was to be born the first week of January, every penny we had was being saved to pay for the doctor and the hospital. I placed ornaments from our first Christmas the year before, in bowls on the table and we celebrated by going to a movie.

The day before New Years, while I was carrying laundry upstairs to wash, I began feeling the first signs of labor. By the time I finished the laundry, I thought it best to call the doctor, who told me to call when the cramps came closer together. I called Will at the hospital where he worked, took a shower and shaved my legs. (Can't have a baby without shaved legs!) By that time, Will was home and the doctor said it was time to come in.

Will showered and dressed in his suit and tie and we headed for the hospital.

❖

I was examined while my pains progressively became more intense. I wanted Will by my side, but they kept chasing him out every time they wanted to examine me. I figured he had as much right to be there as they did, and I *needed* him. But, they had their regulations and they were sticking to them. By late evening, my pains were almost more than I could bear and the nurse was not sympathetic, nor did she allow Will to come in and comfort me. Suddenly, around midnight, everything stopped. No more pains. I slept a few short hours before the pains began to progress again.

I had no idea how much pain I would experience, other than my mother telling me she went to 'death's door' to give birth to me. Now, I had a pretty good idea. Soon, I was begging for something to ease the pain, only for them to remind me that I had chosen *natural* childbirth. Will became upset and sternly told them to forget what I'd said and give me something *now*!

By 12:30 in the afternoon, on New Years' Day, 1957, a year and nine months after we were married, we had our new baby boy, Michael. Looking into this sweet little face, seeing the pucker of his tiny lips and nose, his big dark eyes without brows or lashes; cradling the tiny feet and hands in ours….Will and I were both overwhelmed. Suddenly, aware we were no longer two, but three of us! So much wonder wrapped up in this soft, squirming little bundle.

On bringing him home, everything seemed surreal, even though we had anticipated this coming event for months. I remember waking up in the night. The borrowed crib was standing next to the window with the street lights from outside softly lighting the little mound that lay in it. Then, with just a tiny squeak and grunt I saw this little head rise up. I felt a chill run through me as those big eyes looked straight at me. I think for a second we looked at each other in a strange wonder of *'who are you?'* A new experience for both of us.

❧

In just a few short weeks, after our arrival in California, having a new baby to pay for, on top of a car and rent payments. Will found it necessary to look for a second job as the VA paid merely $250 a month. He found a position as a fry cook at a hamburger place, where he worked evenings and alternate weekends, so we didn't get to see him very much.

However, every available Sunday , we dressed up in our best, and with our little Mike tucked in the seat between us, took a Sunday drive to some new destination. How we enjoyed every spare moment together. Infant seats were not required then, but shortly after he was born, we were able to borrow a car bed that sat on the back seat and was strapped in for safety. The baby was not secured, however.

Driving down Highway 5, past San Jose, continuing south through lovely farm country, we could not get enough of the beautiful sights. The waves of green hills, dotted here and there with trees were so picture perfect. Then we cut over to coastal Highway 101, winding through the trees and finally seeing the ocean appear before us. We found an overlook where we stopped to watch and listen to the waves pounding against the rocky shore. What beauty to behold.

Will often entertained me with stories he had read by Ernest Hemmingway. He wrote about the people in the early 30's who streamed into California from the Midwest fleeing the ravaging destruction of the dust bowl and the aftermath of the great depression.

Now, we were intrigued to see the remaining landmarks of what Hemmingway wrote about in historical Monterey and Carmel.

Our family

Will met a man, a regular customer at the drive-in restaurant who offered him a job in the building maintenance business. The VA hospital job didn't pay as much, so he took this job as part time work. Managing the hamburger shop and working nights at his maintenance job never gave Will much free time. But, when his employer at the hamburger drive-in offered him full time work, he was able to drop the maintenance job as well. We saw a light on our horizon.

Mike was almost three when our second child, Lorna was born in the spring, on May 17, 1960. It had been another joyful pregnancy and now we had a beautiful little girl. What fun it was to receive all sorts of little pink things to dress and swaddle her in. We were now blessed with the perfect family.

Mike was the proud big brother. He was fascinated by how little she was and couldn't quite grasp the fact that she was so delicate. I would often find him in the crib lying along side of her, playing with her toes or hands. He was my helper. While I worked in the kitchen I would tilt the recliner back and lay her in the seat. She was close enough to watch and I knew she could not fall out. One day I heard this little voice behind me say *"Mommy, look what I've got."* As I turned around, there was Mike carrying his baby sister, his arms tightly wrapped around her tummy....... her feet straight up, under his chin and her head was almost touching the floor!

Things became difficult during Will's second year at the hamburger shop. The owner began drinking heavily, making the work environment increasingly difficult.

During this stressful time, I got the mumps. Because of his work situation, Will could not be at home to help much, so he hired a lady from an agency. An older lady in her 60's. We thought she would be able to handle the situation. Since Lorna was still so tiny and Mike knew how to make his own peanut butter sandwich or fix a bowl of cereal, there was really very little for her to do, except supervise Mike and change and feed Lorna. It shouldn't have been too hard for her, however, the lady much preferred telling me about her many romantic liaisons than caring for my children. Because she was too tired to get up to tend the baby at night, I was forced in my feverish misery to stumble out of bed in my delirium to care for my crying infant. So much for our hired nanny! Will let her go the next morning.

A week later, Will got the mumps as well. Here we were with an active three-year-old, a baby girl barely six-weeks-old and both of us in bed, incapable of working. To top things off, his boss was upset that Will took this time off to be sick, and this brought an end to his job.

Recovery came and Will went out looking for work. Intermittently, we enjoyed the free time to go to the beach and other things, but we found ourselves scraping for money. Wills greatest enjoyment was his guns. Occasionally he found someone he could go hunting or target shooting with, but now the time had come when he felt he needed to sell his prized guns so we had money to live. That was a huge sacrifice for him. I knew how much his guns meant to him and hated to see him do it. But, I was very proud of his willingness and sacrifice.

Almost 3 months had gone by before Will was reinstated at the VA Hospital. I got a job at a semi-conductor plant. Line after line of people sat assembly style in front of a microscope and welded minuscule gold beads to tiny transistors that were used in electronics. Eight long hours crept tediously by, night after night of repetitious work that never varied. We chatted with our neighbors on the sly to help the time pass and collected the tiny gold threads that were trimmed off to be discarded to see who collected the biggest wad of scrap.

Will worked early morning to mid afternoon. I worked early to late evenings.

This arrangement allowed one of us to always be at home with the children. It was not easy for me to leave my babies. Lorna was so little then but with Will feeding her, diapering her, caring for her and putting her to bed at night, they built a special bond together and she became Daddy's girl.

On weekends we took long bike rides to the park where the kids could play a while. Then we followed a favorite route on our way back home, down a long hill on Page Mill Road, past the electronic plants. Will and I each had a kiddy carrier on the back of our bikes. Will carried Mike and I had Lorna. Starting at the top of the hill we just let the bikes coast, picking up momentum with each revolution of the wheels until we were riding at a break-neck speed. Mike squealed with delight. What fun that was! Today, I shudder at the consequences we might have paid for such reckless antics. Only by the Grace of God did we keep from crashing!

We continued with our jobs for several months until Will went back to building maintenance again *Full Time*! After the stressful months we had just been through, it was a relief to know I could finally quit working. I was excited to be a stay-at-home mom again. This was cause for celebration so we opened a bottle of wine to commemorate the occasion.

Nine months later, we had a second baby girl!

Lisa came on December 14, 1961. She was our special Christmas baby! The hospital sent the babies home in a big stocking. It was almost unimaginable that we had this little bundle under our tree. The older children could barely keep their hands off of her Although, she was our largest baby, 10 lbs, she fit nicely into Lorna's little doll crib. This intrigued Lorna, only 18-months-old. She had her own real live doll. She liked to sit in the little rocker and hold her baby sister and sing to her, barely more than a baby herself.

The mere 18 months that separated the two girls kept me a very busy mom. Lorna was so little, hovering between infant and toddler stage. When we brought Lisa home Lorna naturally wanted me to pick her up and carry her as I'd done before. But I was warned not to carry anything heavy for a couple weeks, so I complied. This, along with the months I had to leave her to go to work when she was so tiny, was difficult for her. She felt a certain rejection from me. But, as often as I could I would have her climb on my lap and we would spend time reading and cuddling in the rocking chair. Through those early months we formed a routine. I would hold both babies on my lap while I rocked and sang to them. Even Mike, on occasion joined the already crowded lap for a few uncomfortable minutes.

During the time between Will losing his job at the Drive-In and being without work was a challenging time financially. We pinched pennies every way we could. The children were growing out of their clothes. When Lisa was born a few months later, the ladies at the church gave us a baby shower. What a blessing that was. She got so many little dresses and outfits of different sizes. Some that she would not fit into for a year. Yet, since Lorna had a petit frame, many of those things fit her. This provided nice things for both of them to wear.

So many times, I remember how people complimented me on how my children were presented. They noticed how the girls hair was always fixed with pretty ribbons and Mike always looked neat and polished. Often I heard the compliment "They look as if they just stepped off a band box".

We walked to church and the store, Mike on his bike and the little ones in the stroller, simply cutting corners where ever possible.

After Will was steadily employed, we were still pulling ourselves out of months of financial stress. We had been in that position before, but this time we had 3 children to clothe and feed. This was a time we really began to learn to find fun things to do with our family that cost little or nothing. Going to the park, having picnics, bike riding every where we went were a few things we could do together as a family. Will even rode his bike to work. We took the kids to the library every week and many other things, became a weekly routine all the years we were in Palo Alto, I believe we all perceived that time as a special benefit in our memory.

Family Fun

Will made every effort to give us opportunities to enjoy the outdoors. We went to the beach, camping, swimming and took hikes in the woods. We frequented drive-in movie theaters and made occasional trips to the San Francisco Zoo, It was not unusual on waking on Saturday morning for someone to ask, "What are we going to do today?"

We carried a picnic lunch in our back packs where ever we went. I would have to say that the San Francisco Zoo and the beach were our all-time favorites. The best part of visiting the zoo was feeding the animals. The squirrels were entertaining as they scrambled here and there to snatch morsels of food dropped along the walk. Occasionally one was brave enough to climb up on the bench where we sat, eagerly expecting a hand out.

We loved feeding the sea lions raw fish purchased from a nearby vendor. They always drew a big crowd as they eagerly climbed on their perch, begging loudly for their morsel of food. It was fun to watch them fight for the pieces of fish and clap their fins and bark for more.

At the beach the kids immediately began digging holes and carrying pails full of water as the waves washed in. They spent the day building sand castles, jumping waves and burying each other until all you could see were their face and toes. At the end of the day everyone went home happy, sunburned and very tired, still carrying with them remnants of sand that stubbornly clung until we hit the shower.

Palo Alto and the surrounding area offered a wealth of diverse activities for our family to enjoy. There were clay classes for the kids, swimming lessons, preschool classes, and neighborhood recreational activities; always something interesting for every age.

For a time, we had a VW bus that we converted so all of us could sleep in it. We prepared to take the family on a camping trip to Kansas, by way of Disneyland and the Grand Canyon.

Will built a rack on top of the VW and we packed it full of canned goods and all the other necessities for such an adventure. This naturally made the load very heavy. (I guess we didn't think there would be stores along the way and we certainly wanted to be prepared.) However, the engine wasn't powerful enough to take the hills and mountain roads more than 35 miles an hour. We chugged up one hill after another, frustrated, but enjoying the scenery. It might have been helpful if some of us would have offered to get out and push, but we already felt a bit like the Beverly Hillbillies.

On one of our trips to Idaho with this bus, we encountered a rollover just ahead of us in the desert close to the Nevada/Idaho border. We found one man who had been thrown over the fence, now covered with dust, bleeding and seriously injured. The other one had run off. Being an era before cell-phones, passers-by went on ahead to phone for an ambulance, while we waited trying to do what we could.

We covered him with blankets and talked with him to guard against shock for the long hour until help arrived.

This experience made a deep impression on Will. He decided we needed helmets, at least for the front seat passengers. I was dumbfounded at the thought. But no amount of talking would dissuade him.

On our way through Twin Falls that same day, he bought two helmets. We had to wear them if we were in the front seat. This was humiliating for me. Nevertheless, Will was my husband. He wanted to protect us. I chose to respect his decision and reluctantly wore mine, hoping no one would notice. Strangely, though, I do not remember any of the children expressing the desire to ride in the front seat.

This was a most difficult scheme for me to deal with. So to make it more aesthetic, I glued plastic flowers all over mine. Blue-green ones. Swim caps at that time had flowers on them, so I figured flowers on my helmet might make it seem a bit more acceptable. No matter where we went, people would turn their heads to catch a second glance. It was the '60's after all, the age of the "flower child." I still get teased mercilessly about my 'hyped up' flower hat.

The Unexpected

Our life was moving along smoothly. Mike and Lorna were in school and the youngest, Lisa, would be starting very soon. Life was taking on an easier role.

Just when we least expected it, I discovered I was pregnant again. We decided to tell the children on Christmas morning. We hung a tiny baby bootie with the children's Christmas stockings which stirred considerable curiosity. In spite of morning sickness, I enjoyed the children's excitement. All the gifts were opened and the wrapping paper had settled to the bottom of the happy frenzy. Will announced that we had one more present. All eyes lit up in expectancy as he took down the last hanging stocking, a tiny baby one, he announced, "We're going to have another baby! Mommy has a baby in her tummy."

It took a moment for the news to soak in to their heads, then the excitement erupted. Lisa didn't quite understand. Stunned, she came close and moved aside my robe, looking for this strange new baby. "The baby's in there?" She asked, concern furrowing her brow.

"Yes, but its *inside* Mommy's tummy," Will explained. "And its very tiny so you can't see it yet."

"It's going to be a boy!" Mike said, matter of fact, as he stretched to his full height. He was nearly 10. Suddenly assuming a 'big brother' posture and with a hint of command, announced, "It better be a boy. If its not a boy I'm leaving home!"

Will continued, "This is why Mommy isn't feeling very good. She's going to need a lot of rest and we're going to need to help her a lot."

Lorna sprung into action with the doctor kit she had just received and immediately went to work nursing me. She took my pulse and listened to my heart with the real stethoscope we had bought at a medical supply store. She checked my throat with the Popsicle-stick tongue depressor and administered candy pills to ease my 'pain'. This however made me nauseous so, instead she wrapped my arm in a bandage of gauze and tape. All afternoon, she took my vital signs and temperature, never letting me out of her sight for more than a few minutes.

Conveniently, during my pregnancy the PBS station showed a documentary of a child birth. This was fascinating to all of us and answered many of the children's questions.

With every pregnancy, Will made me feel so cherished. He took me shopping and bought outfits for me and treated me like a queen. For every delivery, he dressed in his best suit and tie for taking me to the hospital. I treasure always, this man, dressed in his best, offering his tenderness. Just being in his presence made the birth a most special occasion. He would stay with me as long as he could in the labor, holding my hand, giving me comfort until the time came to be wheeled into the delivery room. Will had a way of making every pregnancy a very special time for me.

It had always been Will's greatest desire to be present for the delivery, but in those days hospital staff frowned on fathers in the delivery room. Each appeal was met with negative responses that made him feel as if his request was improper. Even having worked for two years in a surgical unit didn't qualify him. But in the mid 60's, things were beginning to change. We heard of a new hospital in the area that was allowing this, and our doctor agreed to let me go there. We were both delighted.

On July 28, 1967, Chris came into our lives. Being present at the birth of his little son was a major highlight in Will's life.

What joy when the day finally came and we could bring this tiny baby home. While Will came up to my room to wait for the doctor to come and release me, Mike stayed downstairs in the lobby with his two sisters. During what seemed like an endless time until we were brought down in a wheel chair, they witnessed an unusual and somewhat disconcerting event. A commotion drew their attention to a stark naked woman dashing through the corridor with several hospital personnel running after her.

This was the topic of discussion on the drive home. Oh, they were excited about seeing their baby brother for the first time, there's no doubt about that. However, the exhibit they observed at the hospital did give them a great deal to question.

On each occasion of our children's birth, one of our mothers came to help out, but when Chris was born, Will took a week off of work and stayed with us. I felt so comforted and pampered by having that special loving care from him. At the first cry, he got up in the night, to changed the baby and bring this hungry little bundle to me in bed where he loved to watch him nurse.

It was a special treat for the older children, having Daddy home. During the day, he would take them to a movie, or the park. He always had activities for them so they would feel completely connected as a family.

This little guy brought added blessing to our family. Having a new baby was an exciting time for the children. Mike's request had been honored and he was very excited to finally have his baby brother. He was 10-years-old and took great pride in this cuddly little bundle whom he began to refer to as *"my little pot roast."*

Lorna was seven by then and continued her excellent nursing practices and took good care of me and saw that her baby brother was well cared for. She and Lisa would run back and forth between me and the sleeping baby, giving me minute by minute updates on every move he made. The two 'little mamas' kept their constant vigil over him from the moment we brought him home from the hospital. I knew of every squirm or squeak that came from his crib.

As he grew older, they continued to keep their loving eyes on him. Lisa, now 5, was just beginning kindergarten. She dearly loved school and assumed the role of teacher. She set him down and played school with him whenever he was willing. He loved this attention and became her devoted student.

More Family Adventures

Chris was still tiny when Will bought a truck and camper that slept all of us very comfortably, but there was no place for baby. Once again, Lorna's doll crib was put to use. It fit right into the spot behind the pass through from the camper to the cab. He would be safe there where we could keep an eye on him. Then as he grew we created a crib for him on the floor in the same spot.

In the following years, we traveled to Kansas, Idaho, Grand Canyon, and Disneyland as well as weekend trips to the beach.

A favorite winter camping trip to the snow became an annual event. Leaving the mild Bay Area climate behind, we drove to the snow-covered mountains at Calaveras Big Trees. We spent the weekend tubing and tobogganing down the slopes. We built snow forts and snow men until we were exhausted and frozen stiff. Returning to the cozy camper, we warmed up with hot chocolate and dried out our mittens until we were ready for another round.

When evening came and everyone was wet and cold, we heated up the oven in our camper which made everything warm and cozy in a hurry. We peeled off the wet clothes, hung them on a line strung overhead, and got comfortable. More hot cocoa while dinner was cooking and playing a game of some sort before laying out the sleeping bags for a good nights rest.

Will loved the outdoors. It was his desire to introduce his first backpacking adventure to Mike when he was 13. I'm thinking, perhaps, this was Wills first backpacking trip as well. I know he spent a lot of time studying on it through outdoor magazines and catalogs.

It was a 3-mile hike to Sardine Lake in the mountains of Yosemite National Park. They told us of the beautiful snow-capped peaks that surrounded the lake, where the days were warm and lazy and the fish jumped all day long in the icy cold water.

Exhilarated by the adventure, Will was certain that backpacking would make a great family outing. I was reluctant, but Will's heart was so in this. He talked about nothing else. How could I refuse?

A venture like this takes an enormous amount of planning and preparation. We would be camping for six days, which meant we needed enough food for six people for that length of time; plastic containers and purifying pellets for drinking water, cooking utensils, and first-aid supplies. Each one of us was outfitted with fishing gear, proper clothing, boots, bedding, and sleeping bags. Among other necessities were waterproof tent covers, hatchets, and plenty of matches. The list was endless and it all had to go into three large packs, so it was important to keep careful watch on the overall weight.

The whole family was involved in the preparations for this adventure. Will and Mike began welding frames of light-weight tubing together for enough backpacks for all six of us. While the guys made frames, I sewed a backpack to match Will's professional *Kelty* pack. This was a new challenge for me and I dared anyone to compare the quality! I also made a little down sleeping bag for Chris. Will took such pride in making this a family effort. He often said, "it was a dream come true."

All the preparation had built anticipation for each of us until we couldn't wait to begin. The air was filled with excitement that glorious July morning when we donned our backpacks and took our first steps. The two young girls carried trail food in their pack along with their own sleeping bags. Chris, only three-years-old, carried his own little sleeping bag strapped to his back. Like a trooper, he marched right along the trail. For only one short stretch, Will carried him on his shoulders.

The scenery was breath taking and we were all alone in the 'wilderness.' Although we girls worried about bears, Will taught us how to hang our food supplies high in a tree to discourage their invasion and we never encountered a one. We ate the fish we caught every day and cooked over the open fire. As the warm days cooled into the dark night, the sky became vibrant with brilliant stars the city skies only hinted of. We huddled together around the fire sipping hot chocolate and roasting marshmallows. There's nothing like a cozy fire against the deep darkness that draws a family together. They were beautiful moments that would serve as an anchor for our family when the stresses of city life would attempt to swallow us. For the moment, the city was far away and we felt very close to each other.

The nights were long, trying to sleep on a thin pad with the hard ground under me. And did you ever notice when you are cold, your bladder called for relief more frequently? That's when I would wake Will to take me for a short walk, to protect me from a lurking bear or whatever the darkness might hold. Returning, I buried my head down into the sleeping bag again to get warm. Still far from the comforting warmth of my soft bed at home, my aching bones told me that morning had not come any too soon. Feeling the chill air as I crawled out of my sleeping bag, the strong aroma of coffee tantalized my nostrils. Greeting us with his usual cheery "Good Morning", Will was already leaning over the blazing fire stirring up pancake batter and roasting some of yesterdays catch for our breakfast.

We all pitched in here and there, but Will had taken on the major tasks of camping. Whether it was planning, cooking, cleaning fish, because he wanted me to enjoy it as much as he did, he basically treated me as his guest.

Will and Mike planned all winter long for their next major backpacking event. One particular summer, they viewed the world at 14,495 ft from the peak of Mt Whitney. The younger children and I stayed behind at our base camp next to a stream where we could enjoy playing in the shallow water.

Year after year, Will made sure our family experienced memorable adventures together. Things that he had missed out on when he was growing up. Will's family never seemed to take time to play. He had never been fishing or did any mountain hiking, so having these experiences together with our children was very important to him.

Will decided a canoe was something we could take on our camping trips. Our first adventure out in the canoe was on Lake Berryessa, a large body of water in Northern California. Everyone got safety vests and fishing gear and together we took to the water. The clouds moved in, a bitter cold wind picked up, and the water became very choppy. I was suppose to paddle into the waves to keep it from tipping while Will baited the hooks for the kids to fish. I did not know a thing about paddling a canoe and the waves were whipping at us. I couldn't keep the canoe pointed in the right direction. I was scared and yelling for help. It was not a happy start. Finally sensing the danger, Will gave up the fishing lesson, took the paddles and headed us back to shore. Once we were safely on shore and warming up in our camper, I for one, decided from now on, I would settle only for glassy smooth water no deeper than I could stand up in.

Still, on better, calmer, sunnier days, we often took the canoe to Foothill Lake just a few miles from Palo Alto. Once we ventured as far as Tioga Lake in the Tuolumne Meadows, a south eastern part of Yosemite National Park. Here the water was still and clear, offering a perfect place for kids to learn canoeing in natures beauty.

Life in the 60's

Will was working 14-hour days supervising the cleaning and maintenance of 60 banks. His work began at 5pm and would stretch into the late morning. This meant that family time was scarce on weekdays, often dinner being the only time together before Will went out again to work another 12 hours or so. As the kids got older he attempted to fill that void by giving each one an occasional opportunity to accompany him to work.

There came a time, however, when going to the bank was unsafe even for Will. This was a time in the '60s when the Black Panthers, the Weathermen and other Free Rights radicals inspired by Malcolm X were threatening to bomb businesses, particularly banks. Major cities throughout the country were inundated with riots and hate gatherings protesting the Vietnam War. Law enforcement officers risked their lives and many paid the ultimate prices in attempts to maintain peace. The whole country was on the verge of chaos. Palo Alto was no different. In fact, with Stanford University within a mile of our home, we found ourselves in a very volatile environment.

For a season, demonstrations would break out with loud shouting, occasional gun shots and glass breaking, even cars being set on fire. Even on calm nights the air was thick with the threat of violence and the on-going risk of a bank bombing. It was into this atmosphere that Will ventured night after night to perform his work duties, while we, his family, remained safe and secure in our little home. Thankfully, he and the banks he serviced escaped harm in the middle of this war.

Mike was a junior in high school at this time and eager for adventure. He was earning money with a paper route and working with Will on Sundays. His desire for independence was pushing against the boundaries of his world. He took his bicycle to parks, to the bay across town, to the games at Stanford University - everywhere he and his friends wished to go. I thought it was important for our son to have a curfew.

Most of his friends were from single-parent homes and had no structure in their lives. I began speaking to Will about this, trying to point out that this could lead to possible trouble. I guess you could say I began nagging Will on this subject.

They often played basketball at the school just across the street from where we lived, sometimes until late at night. So one night he walked over to the school, I thought to bring Mike home. But it was very, very late when they came home, both in high spirits. Will had gone over and played with them that entire time. I know I scolded Will for that, but eventually, I understood his wisdom in the matter.

This was the time in a young man's life, when he needed to interact with his father, man to man. Something that Will had missed as he was growing up. They began doing more things together and began exploring Mike's fascination with motorcycles. Will and Mike shopped for used motor bikes, tore them apart and reassembled them. Putting the pieces of the bikes together seemed to bring them together.

Parenting can be an overwhelming experience. You look at a newborn and think of this little life that you are responsible to bring up to his full potential. Thankfully you don't have to worry about what college they will attend at this point in time. All you have to do is love them and be there for them, attend to the little matters that occur from day to day

Will and I were not ideal parents… not even close! We learned right along with our children, what works and what didn't. Many times, as they grew older, it might have been easier to throw in the towel, but we reminded ourselves we'd signed up for the long haul.

We found that many of the same principles of marriage apply to raising kids. Listening to their needs and ideas and giving them the same respect you give your spouse are possibly the most important. But we didn't learn that all at once. It took many years.

The challenges began small. Then one day, I found myself, in a face to face conflict with Mike. Once the tiny infant I held in one hand, now was 5 feet tall with a mouth and ideas as large as the Grand Canyon. Here I was, not so different from where I started, save a few gray hairs showing up here and there, now finding myself completely out-sized and not sure what to do next.

A time when Will's mother was visiting, I found myself again butting heads with my son. After the encounter, I threw up my hands and wearily proclaimed, "I just don't know what to do with that kid. He just doesn't listen to me!" I'll never forget what Will's mother said to me that day.

"You don't have to do anything. Just love him."

That's all? As I thought this over, I began to see that I had not been listening to him, nor did he listen to me. If

I showed respect, by listening to his opinion, the door to discussion might open, rather than be slammed shut in a fury of judgment. I began trying this and found how much easier we interacted with each other. It didn't happen over night.

It had to be a day to day event. For us, it took a long time, but in the process we both matured and our relationship grew stronger, easier, and more precious!

Just as most parents do from the time the children were little, Will and I made promises to each other and ultimately to them. We would bring them up to respect themselves and others, to take pride in their values and to be who they were destined to be. This is a tall order for parents, and we found out how difficult it is to carry those promises through when the rubber hits the road. Yet, by persisting and instructing them day by day toward that goal, it's amazing what comes together. Now that they are grown I look at them with such pride and admire them for who they are.

We both made so many mistakes, but over the years since, we've talked with our children, asked forgiveness where we were wrong and just plain stupid at times. The children have graciously forgiven us. I cannot emphasize enough, the importance of talking through the hurts.

Will and I acquired some very important insights in our relationship with our children. We learned the importance of having fun together as a family; listening rather than judging; respecting them and teaching them to respect us, and instilling the values that would help them make good choices in life. Perhaps the most difficult was learning to step back, allowing them the space to make their own mistakes and work them out themselves.

Will and I loved our children so dearly. Because we believed wholeheartedly that marriage is for life, we determined that when they brought home the person they wanted to spend their life with, we would enfold that person into our family with the same love and respect as one of our own.

It's amazing to see the long road from infancy into adulthood unfold. When they stand before you no longer a child but a fellow adult, you look at them with deep pride and respect for who they have become. I observe how they interact with their own children, how they handle conflicts with grace and wisdom, I can't help but wish I'd have understood how to be like that.

Our family is truly one to be proud of. Will and I have admired them and often said to each other as we looked proudly at the entire group, *"this is what you and I made!"*

Our Wedding April 10, 1955

Will 'n Joan

Grampa 'n Heather

Grampa 'n Shandra

Break Time

Table Talk w/Jenny 'n Jonas

Katie fishin' with Grampa

Master Craftsman

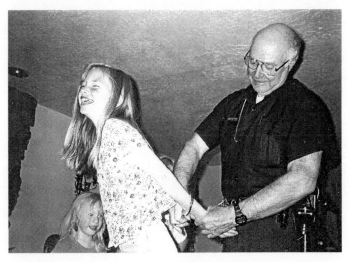

Yer¹ Under Arrest

Still in Love at 48 years.

A Time of Decision

......choose you this day whom you will serve
.....but as for me and my house, we will serve the LORD.
Joshua 24:15

We were both brought up by parents who were devout believers in the Christian faith. They took us to church, taught us right from wrong and instilled a belief system in us.

However, at the age of 20, when Will left the guarded grace of his childhood home, he began to realize there were many kinds of beliefs and this brought questions to his mind. In comparison, they differed from what he had been taught. He began to wonder how God related to him as an individual.

It began with his growing frustration of the dogmatic religious upbringing of his youth. He grew frustrated with cultural wars over religion around the world and certain inconsistencies he observed within the churches in general. These became a source of confusion in his life. The formal, ritualistic church service seemed lifeless to him,. This, combined with what he saw as a judgmental, intolerant attitude of people who referred to themselves as Christian's, just didn't seem to add up. He came to reject his spiritual upbringing and, for a number of years, he considered himself an agnostic. It wasn't that he had stopped believing in God; it was just that God didn't seem to exist in his neighborhood.

He was eager for knowledge and for answers to his own life questions. Curiosity about different cultures and religions created more questions about God and mortality in general. He ventured into a long search through reading books on different cultures and different walks of life.

I can never recall a time when Will did not reflect the character of God in his life. Although he would tell you that for nearly 20 years he rejected the religious aspect of God. If God really existed, what did it have to do with him? He was a good person. This was evident. This led him to tell God not to bother him anymore.

In spite of this confusion about God and how He fit into Will's life, there were times that he did reach out to God. On occasion, when my mother was seriously ill or when our children were ill from time to time, he didn't hesitate to offer a prayer with me in their behalf. I had found a church within walking distance from where we lived in Palo Alto. Will worked most Sundays and he had no interest in church, but he always supported my attendance with our children. He enjoyed going to church parties with me and attended the children's programs, but that's where he drew the line.

He continued to be interested in the supernatural and had a avid curiosity about intelligent life in other worlds. When Will was a young boy of around 11 or 12, he saw a large cone shaped object hovering in the sky over the American Falls Reservoir. He kept his eyes on it for some time. It never changed shape and continued to remain in one place until suddenly it vanished. He never forgot this and spoke of it quite often, but no one else claimed to see it. Although folks down-played the story of what he saw that day, his interest never wavered.

Years later he read a series of books by an author, Erich von Däniken who wrote about UFOs in one of several books called "Chariots of the Gods." His theory considered the technology of the aliens to be supernatural and the aliens themselves to be gods. He interprets Ezekiel's revelation in the Old Testament as a detailed description of a landing spacecraft.

After reading these books, Will was eager to discuss this with various church scholars. These views always shocked and flabbergasted Christians who flatly falsified whatever he said, instantly slamming the door to further discussion.

This fascination culminated when he became acquainted with the pastor of the church our kids and I attended. One evening when Will went to pick up our girls from youth group, he had a chance meeting the pastor who happened to be in the foyer. Pastor Ron introduced himself. Knowing the kids had been praying for their father and meeting him for the first time, peaked an interest. From that point, he set out to befriend Will.

They met for breakfast on a weekly basis and Will began sharing *his* views of religion and his idea of UFO's being heavenly visitors to us. Ron did not put him down for his ideas! He listened to what Will had to say. He spoke of his own spiritual search during his youth and told what he found to be truth. Will was immediately drawn to this man who showed respect for his views, even when they differed from the truth he had come to accept. This mutual respect developed into a deep friendship. Still for a time Will kept his distance from church.

A short while into this relationship, Ron told Will about a guy who would be speaking at church on "Ezekiel and the Flying Saucers." When Will heard that someone would actually speak on UFO's at church, his interest was awakened. His mind was set to go and hear this, although he said nothing to me. The following Sunday morning, when he would normally be at work, he was home in the shower.

"What are you doing in the shower," I asked. "Are you finished with your work, already?"

"No," he replied. " I'm going to church with you." All went quiet. I was stunned!

I didn't want to question him too much, for fear he would "chicken out," but this was the beginning of connecting the dots for him. Very soon, he began to open his mind to the possibility that God was for real and that this gift of freedom and fullness of life was for him. Something he had never before experienced.

Ron and Will embraced what would evolve into a lifetime of brotherly affection for each other. Will often reflected on this time, for years to come. "Ron is the only one who would ever listen to me without putting me down!" he would say with amazement.

Ron remembers a very special Sunday evening service. He was on the platform when he observed a sparkle of joy on Lorna's face. She and Lisa had been praying with the youth group for some time, asking that their father would see God for who He really wanted to be in his life. *"Then"* Ron says, *" I looked over to Will, and I'll never forget as long as I live; like a dark shadow moved from across his face and his whole countenance lit up. It was such a beautiful thing to see."*

There was nothing earth shaking that happened. He was just ready to open his mind to God. It was simply a change of heart.

Will had all the outer qualities of a great person, but in his heart he lacked the personal relationship with God. When he opened his heart and mind to receive God's offer of freedom, he discovered that any past guilt and self-condemnation had gone, giving him a confidence that made his spirit lighter. God's Spirit began to guide him, giving him a deeper understanding of God's plan for his life. Through this restored connection with God, new avenues began opening to him, giving his life new meaning and purpose.

This change in Will's heart gave him a renewed spiritual responsibility for his family and introduced a new dynamic for us. Mike, 16 years old now, felt confusion over the sudden change in the atmosphere of our home and didn't know how this would effect him. Although Will tried to explain it to him, he didn't understand. He worried that he would be rejected by us in some way or that we would demand things from him that he was not ready for. But in time we could see him relax, feeling less threatened. He began to hang around when our friends or the teen group came to our house.

At this same time, Pastor Ron saw the need for a special TLC group for those of us new believers. We were invited to come with our attitudes, angers, fears, questions or whatever baggage we were carrying around. No pretenses allowed!

There was a couple in their 80's who had attended a large prestigious church all their lives but didn't know God could be a personal part of them. There were recovering alcoholics who needed new friends, a Jewish gal on drugs who often came stoned and then there was Will and I. We were just a collection of misfits who wanted God, but not the formality of church. We needed a place where we could be real. Ron just let us talk about our 'stuff' and prayed with us and showed us how to pray for each other. We loved coming there because we could be open with one another. Nothing anyone said could shock us. We were accepted just as we were or what mood we were in.

There were little things in his own life that Will began to feel did not model a clear representation of God. Yet there is one time that stands out. One which Will often spoke of as a turning point in his life. One that I will always remember, for it cut a deep impression into me.

It was a lovely Saturday. Will didn't have to work, so he had invited me to spend the whole afternoon with him. We would do something special together ~ lunch, shopping or whatever we wanted. It would be a fabulous day! There was only one problem, his boss had a supervisors meeting scheduled for the morning. That would only take an hour or two and he promised to be home to pick me up at noon. Excited, I got the kids settled into their activities for the day, then I focused on getting ready for a date with my husband.

Noon came. I watched eagerly for him to come through the door. 12:30 came.

1 o'clock came...still no sign of Will. I took into consideration that the meeting had taken a bit longer and tried to calm my anxious mind. But why didn't he call? 2 o'clock came, then 3. 4 o'clock and no Will! By now, I was frantic. I was worried something could have happened to him. *'Why hadn't he called? Where was he? Did he forget about our plans?'* I thought of so many things that could have happened. *'But he always calls if he will be late'*, I reminded myself, and worried some more.

Finally, the door opens. He walked in, all smiles, happy, and gleefully grinning from ear to ear!

"Hi, honey," he greeted cheerfully. Cheerful was *not* what I was ready for!

I was ready for deep remorse, apologies, begging for mercy! And all I got was this happy-go-lucky guy! He was sauced! Completely and totally drunk!

"How could you?" I pleaded. "You promised." "You didn't even call!" I had more... much more to say, but....

He eagerly proceeded to tell of his meeting with the guys Believing that I would enjoy his rendition of the eventful morning and how many drinks they shared. They had began with a few, then broke into a case of wine...

I couldn't listen to more. I could not believe his joyful attitude when I was deeply hurt. I grabbed the keys and ran out! He followed me to the car.

"Where are you going?" he asked

"I'm running away!" I wailed.

"Can I come with you?" he asked, sweetly, as he opened the side door and got in.

Silently, I drove up Page Mill Road, into the hills that overlooked the city and finally pulled over and stopped.

"I wasn't sure, if you were going to leave me there or drive us off of a cliff," he told me later.

Believe me, the idea had crossed my mind! Instead I got out of the car. Seeing him following me, I climbed a tree and sat there trying to escape him while still being within reach. He approached very sweetly, proclaimed that he was sorry and tried to charm me into coming down.

Slowly, as the effects of alcohol wore off, the impact of this event settled into his mind. The boss and his wife were leaving for Europe the next day, so as this meeting commenced and the major issues were out of the way, it turned into more of a celebration.

Time vanished, reality became obscure. After emptying multiple bottles of expensive wine, the four employees made their departure. Will, drove through heavy traffic, making one or two business stops on the way, and miraculously managed to get home without incident. Until now......

On assessing his behavior, he realized this was not the kind of person he was. He realized not only had he acted irresponsibly, but had broken a promise to me. For this he was deeply repentant.

He never had indulged in that kind of behavior before. Will became sensitive to what kind of message this would send to those he cared about, and to our children who were looking to us as examples to follow.

There were other things Will began to feel needed to be changed in his life.

We had begun associating with a couple, from our TLC class who were just as new to church as Will was. They were giving up their time at bars and trying to overcome alcoholism. They had no friends, other than their drinking buddies, so Will and I invited them to our home.

It came as a surprise to me when Will opened the cupboard one day and began pouring all the liquor down the drain. I couldn't believe it! It seemed like such a waste. Will usually got a bottle or two as a gift at Christmas from a client and they would sit in the cupboard, untouched, for most of the year. Drinking wasn't a problem in our home. But Will wanted to be a support to our friends, partnering with them in cutting alcohol out of their lives.

Many nights we sat in our living room with these friends, drinking coffee until the wee hours of the morning talking about God and our lives. Meanwhile the children, theirs and ours, found a spot to curl up and sleep after they had exhausted all the games. We made many memories together with this family.

Jim formed a group of gospel singers and we enjoyed listening to their practice sessions and became their most faithful fans, following them to their performances and developing a deep friendship and spiritual support. But the alcohol had taken its toll. Jim died a few years later, due to liver disease.

Changes did not come all at once. But over a period of time, as Will's heart drew closer to God, he became aware there were things in his life that did not agree with God's plan.

Something that had troubled Will most of his life, he now realized was not acceptable to God. These were lustful thoughts toward other women. He had tried to battle it alone, but knew now that he must give this over to God. Also, for years he had collected Playboy Magazines. One day the Lord brought this to his mind, reminding him he needed to be a responsible model for his sons. He quickly invited Ron over and they destroyed them together, putting one more thing of the past behind him. Not only did this give Will freedom from guilt, but gave me a whole new confidence in my husband's fidelity. This in turn released me from the painful jealousy and insecurity that had haunted me for so many years.

Greener Pastures

Will had dreamed of returning to Idaho from time to time. The saying, "You can take the boy from the farm, but you can't take the farm from the boy" proved true. His parents had gotten very old and health issues had taken their toll. When they died the family came together to settle the estate.

It was the parent's wish, and everyone agreed, that the home and land be divided between the two sons. Will's brother purchased the two thousand acres of desert land and we purchased the homestead that included the house, a barn and 200 acres of land. Taking ownership of his boyhood home ignited a new spirit of adventure in Will. Not only did he feel drawn to his home roots, but he hoped he could build a closer relationship with his brother who also lived near there.

We knew it would be a while before we could make our transition from California to Idaho. We took several family trips over the next two years to work on the farm.

The first step in Will's plan was to begin cleaning up the place. Crumbling old out- buildings that had accumulated over half a century and dilapidated fences needed to be torn down. So when summer came, he and Mike packed the pickup with all the tools needed to accomplish the job, while the girls and I packed the car with food and clothes for the trip to Idaho.

Mike had recently earned his drivers license so he drove the pickup with Lorna and Lisa taking turns riding with him. Chris, just 5-years-old rode with us in the car. The agreement was that we would keep within sight of each other at all times, should any trouble arise.

Driving the stretch of road between Reno, Nevada and Idaho was long. Miles and miles of lonely desert stretched endlessly with little to see other than sage brush, bare hills, dry grass and a lone rabbit running here or there. Without air conditioning in either vehicle, the summer heat began making everyone tired, thirsty and needing a break. We stopped in Lovelock, for a late lunch and to stretch our legs.

After a brief rest, it was time to hit the road again. Will told Mike to go ahead of us and we would be right behind. He and Lisa drove off, but for some reason we were delayed a bit. Ready to go, I took the wheel and once on the road again, we looked for the pickup. We didn't see it, and thinking they were just a couple of minutes ahead of us, we didn't feel the need to worry. We would catch up soon.

Will had taken a little snooze in the back seat while I drove. As usual, his snoozes were very short. He sat up, looking over my shoulder and asked if I'd seen any sign of the pickup.

"I see them way up ahead of us," I told him. He relaxed for a while and then asked again. The pickup was only a small spot in the distance, further away than before. This made Will nervous so he told me to speed up, which I did, but we were not catching up. The spot was not coming nearer.

"Drive faster," he said, clearly, quite agitated now. " Mike should not be driving that fast. I told him to keep within the speed limit!"

So I drove faster and faster with each of Will's commands. By this time, I was breaking every speed limit in the state Still it was not fast enough for Will.

"Pull over. Let me drive." He said impatiently.

I don't know how fast he drove, but I'm sure we were flying low off the ground, intent on catching up with our kids.   Still, we never came closer to the vehicle in the distance.

Eventually, we began questioning….could it be possible that it wasn't Mike ahead of us after all? The vehicle ahead was so far down the road and there was no way to identify what kind. By this time our frustration gave way to worry. *Could it be that Mike and Lisa were behind us? Could they have had a break-down? What?* Here we were in the middle of the Nevada desert, nothing but hot miles between us and no way to communicate. We had lost our children! There was a sick feeling in the pit of our stomachs. Then all the "what ifs" crowded into our minds. We prayed…oh, yeah, we prayed! *"Where could they be?" "Lord, Keep them safe!"*

Lovelock was now more than a hundred miles behind us and we had not seen our children in over 2 hours. This was very alarming. Then Will spotted a small oasis with a gas station just ahead. As he let up on the accelerator he saw a phone booth near the entrance. No cell phones in those days! Will pulled up to it and called the highway patrol, describing the pickup and our children who were driving it.

We breathed a sigh of relief and sent up a silent prayer of thanksgiving when we learned that no accidents had been reported...Still what could have happened to them?

As the hot sun beat down on us, we anxiously waited by the pay phone for what seemed an eternity. Finally, when that phone rang, we all jumped to attention. It was the highway patrol, telling Will that the lost had been found nearly 100 miles back. They were fine. They hadn't even realized they were lost!

We cheered and laughed in relief. We all relaxed having heard the good news. When they arrived an hour or so later, we were eager to sort out this puzzle.

Mike had made a quick stop at a store in Lovelock, to pick up something to munch on and told Lisa to keep careful watch for us in case we drove by. Lisa didn't see us so they went back to where we had eaten lunch. We were not there. Well, they speculated that we may have just past them and kept driving but still not seeing us, they drove even slower to let us catch up with them. While we were thinking just the opposite and drove faster and faster, they drove slower, putting many miles between us.

With the mystery solved, with sighs of relief, shouts of laughter, hugs and happy to be together again, we continued our journey.

The delay took up a large part of our afternoon, so when we reached Elko, we pulled into a nice motel. Everyone was ready for a good dinner, time to relax and have some fun, as well as a good night's sleep. From here we would be able to finish our trip easily the next day.

City Folks' Summer Adventures

Over the many years, so much on the farm had been neglected. We all got to work. Will and Mike with some help from Chris began tearing down broken corrals, fences and old buildings that no longer served a purpose. One of Mikes friends came up from California and spent a few days. He drove the tractor hauling wagon loads of debris to the dump.

Will and Mike tore down the old broken-down pump house. This was an old leaning shack where old tools and oil cans were stored. *Scattered* is a better way to describe it. Oil spills collected on the dirt floor over the years and somewhere in this rubble was the hole to our water supply. Needless to say, this project was on the priority list.

Rebuilding was a major task. This involved mixing their own cement, laying cinder block, rebar and lava rock to give it the same appearance as the barn. Inexperienced as they were at building a structure, it was a building they could be proud of.

The girls and I chopped weeds, and hauled them to a burn pile. Since the house had set empty for so long, we went through, room by room, cleaning out drawers, running into cobwebs and spiders, and mouse nests. We became very cautious of what we might encounter.

Mice seemed to be everywhere. The live ones could scurry away, but the dead ones lurked in dark and unexpected places. The house filled with screams of terror each time a dead mouse was found folded into old bedding, or swimming in an old bucket with a few inches of stale water. The biggest shock of all was a dead black bird behind a canister in the kitchen, bringing back the memory of the haunting tale of The Raven….*now, how could that have gotten in*?

"You will *not* believe this….." or, "Guess what we found?" was the beginning of so many stories we told the guys who were working outside. We all laughed; marveling at the unexpected that was being discovered.

Best of all were the discoveries of what kinds of interesting things Grandma collected. Newspaper clippings from years gone by, long out-dated sewing notions, hair accessories, old ladies hats and Christmas ornaments; objects of Will's childhood that triggered yet another story. The variety of old treasures went on and on.

The basement was the greatest challenge. Cupboards still filled with Grandma's canned goods. Rows of beans, tomatoes and applesauce along with empty canning jars stood half-hidden under spider webs and dust that also entombed the occasional mouse that had found it's demise. The shelf life of the canned goods was questionable so we took them out to the field where we poured the contents into a hole we had dug. We held a sobering moment, thinking of all the hard work that grandma had put into stock piling this food for her family. And now it had come to this.

There seemed no end to cleaning up the old abandon house. We girls looked at each other and wondered how it was possible to make this a place we could live in the style we'd been accustom to! We had our doubts, but with determination we moved forward.

It was a hard two weeks, but the challenge of the work and the fresh Idaho air, seemed to put everyone in good humor. Most of all, seeing our family working together stirred a deep sense of pride in both Will and myself.

❧

Along the east of the house was an old apple orchard that held many fascinations, not only for the children but for us older ones as well. A small boy and his friends could fill endless hours playing games within those woods. Childhood memories brought a special yearning into his heart as Will was able to pass them on now to his own youngest son, Chris.

In one corner, deeply camouflaged by fallen trees, sat a broken down building that held a random collection of old wagon wheels. Big wheels, little wheels, some wooden, some metal, scraps from farm implements and old chicken feeders all twisted into a rubble. It was a jumble of discarded kitchen items, old porcelain door knobs, skeleton remains of animals hanging from the ceiling, an old chamber pot and bed pan, all covered with cobwebs. It took a bit of bravery to climb over and through this eerie accumulation, with cautiously stepping to avoid tripping and landing on something dead. But the treasures never ceased to intrigue us and the hunts would continue for years to come.

The interesting story of this little building was it's name and origin. 'The Little Red House' now faded and near collapse, was originally known as the 'Summer Kitchen.' A half-century earlier it had set next to the house. In years past, when the Harder family came to Idaho, the original part of the house was a very small stone and concrete building. The kitchen, living and sleeping area was combined into

Joan Saner Harder

the downstairs portion. In the summertime, when there would be field hands to feed along with a large family, this little red house was built to hold a cook stove and other food preparation needs. In time, an addition was built on to the stone house and the 'summer kitchen' was moved into the orchard. There it was used to house a family of farm workers and later was abandoned.

180

Apple Picking Time

It was the autumn of the following year, apple picking time, when we again returned to Idaho. Chris had just recovered from a tonsillectomy and was full of energy.

Will and Mike trimmed dead wood from the apple trees. Chris helped pull debris into a giant burn pile which towered above our heads. Willow sticks were cut while the girls and I brought out wieners and marshmallows to roast. When the time finally came to strike the match, the monstrous inferno drew primal shouts from our throats in celebration and release from the grueling labor.

The girls and I had spent the time preparing the house. The trees in the orchard were loaded with fruit. We brought empty jars up from the basement, scrubbed them by hand and scalded them so we could preserve the abundant supply of ripe apples. This kept us busy for days. One of us filled the jars with applesauce, while another rolled out pie crusts and filled them. Soon the pungent smells of delicious hot spicy pie drifted outside, luring the men inside for a treat.

Chris was an all-around helper and found plenty of fascinating things to keep a 6-year-old busy. One of his jobs was to carry buckets of apples to the house for us to process. Our family enjoyed coming here from time to time, working, playing and making this our home away from home. We began forming pictures in our minds of actually making this our permanent home.

It would be a while before we could make our transition from California to Idaho. After all the hard work we had already put into it, we didn't want to leave the house sitting empty, so we thought the best thing we could do was to touch up the inside of the house and prepare it to use as a rental until the time that we were ready to make our move. We gave the bathroom a bit of a facelift and secured some of the antiques left from Will's parents by locking them away in the upper bedrooms.

After much persuasion, I had managed to convince my mother to fly out from Kansas to join us. I knew she would love it there, but getting her to fly was the challenge. She insisted she couldn't fly. Her heart couldn't take it, she'd say, and a hundred other excuses. But with a few reminders that she needed a little practice before she took her 'flight with the angels,' she agreed.

The day we picked my mother up from the airport, the pressure pump to the well gave out. It had to be replaced so the well had to be "pulled." The 30-foot cylinder that kept the water clean as it was drawn had to be removed in order to replace it with a submersible pump. It was a tedious job that consumed precious time we had not planned for. Our hurried 50-mile trip to Pocatello netted a new pump and a slightly rattled Grandma fresh off her first flight.

She soon found herself in her element, however, as these problems were all too familiar to her. She was eager to help in any way she could. She knew all about conserving water that had to be hauled in from the neighbors. She lent a hand holding the flashlight for Will as he worked in the well hole replacing the pump. Even the old 'out house' had to be put into service, something she'd been doing all her 78 years. This certainly did not phase her. This was 'farm life' to her. She felt right at home. Observing her composure inspired us to take it all in stride.

Our dear friends, Pastor Ron and Alberta had moved to Nampa, Idaho. They came to spend a few days helping us panel the living room to cover up the crumbling plaster. The laughter, the cheerful bantering, and joy that vibrated around us in the midst of hard work was most encouraging and soon we were ready to advertise the place for rent and return to California.

Renting, however, turned into a disaster. Living so far away, it was impossible to monitor the upkeep of the place. We screened the rental applicants as carefully as we could and finally placed our trust in a couple we had checked out quite extensively. Since we would be so far away, we needed someone to look out for the place. Will's brother ran cattle in our pasture, so he made an agreement with his brother to keep a close scrutiny on it for us.

Rent payments soon slipped behind and finally ceased all together. Unpaid utility bills stacked up. When the electric company shut off the power, they disappeared altogether. No matter who we spoke with, no law enforcement who read our report knew anything of them. They were never heard from again.

Preparing For the Big Move

The memories of our time in Idaho had become more inviting as our time in the city stretched into another year. Our thoughts were drawn to the amazing Idaho sunsets, where the stars shined bright in the clear night air, so clear sometimes we could see the Northern Lights dancing and pulsating on the horizon as the world grew quiet. In that world one didn't hear the rumble of traffic or sirens in the distance, only the steady chirp of crickets filling the air with a soothing lullaby and the haunting song of the coyote as it sang to it's little ones. Occasionally the distant call of the sand hill crane, or an owl hooting in the orchard broke through the silence. Sounds of the night gave comfort in the stillness that surrounded our home in the country. Memories of those sounds beckoned us.

Two sales had fallen through for our California house before we finally closed on a third. It was an incredible relief to at last be free to pursue our dreams. Since it would be early November before the transition could be made, Lorna and Lisa had been invited to stay with Will's brother so they could start the new school year in mid-August. They began their 8th and 10th grades in Idaho.

Will would need to finalize his job and all the necessary closures so he sent me up along with Mike and Chris in mid-October to put the house in order and bring our girls back to California for our big move.

When we arrived, Lorna and Lisa came running out to meet us, their arms outstretched, giggling with excitement. Such homesick girls, you've never seen! The volume of exhilaration and laughter, everyone talking at the same time, enough to crack the sound barrier, was normal behavior for our family. We were overjoyed to see each other again.

The kids and I couldn't wait to get over to the farm the next day and be a family again. Eager to begin preparing the house for the arrival of our personal possessions and our new life in Idaho.

We had always left the house in perfect order each time we came for a visit. We knew the house would need some TLC after being rented, then empty for several months, but nothing...*nothing* could have prepared us for what we saw as we drove into the yard......

We found ourselves aghast at the scene that greeted us. Weeds, waist to shoulder height, the front door open and hanging lopsided on a broken hinge, pieces of furniture stood amongst the tall grass in the yard. The refrigerator was found in the barn, the inside crawling with maggots from food left to rot. Inside the house, the putrid odor was so intolerable, we covered our mouth and nose with our hand. Windows had been left wide open for animals and birds to come and go. Leaves had blown in, covering random piles of animal feces. Dead mice were swimming in a half-filled washing machine. A casserole rotted in the oven with a thick layer of mold. In the basement, old boards that clearly were taken from the old outhouse now lay strewn helter skelter.

Oddly, our old family photos were tacked to the boards in some kind of macabre display.

The bathroom told it's own story. It was obvious that a large animal had been locked inside. Deep grooves had been scratched into the walls and door. Filth covered every surface and the toilet was filled with fecal waste. The fixtures were stained a dark filthy brown.

Along with this first inspection, we found the door to the attic had been broken down. All of our antique treasures….gone!

As we later learned from a neighbor, the tenants had backed up a big moving van to the house. They broke into the secured storage, loaded up our personal belongings along with the family antiques and drove off with their plunder. Ironically, they drove their big van loaded with our belongings right up to Will's brothers house to deliver the key, but he had no idea they were driving off with the family heirlooms and some of our most treasured possessions.

I wanted to cry! I was angry! How could this have happened? Why were we not told?   The house had been completely trashed and had set this way for months!

We were so unprepared to find this nightmare starring us in the face. How I wished Will was here with us. He would know what to do and how to handle it. I longed for his comfort. Between sobs, I tried describing this devastating discovery to him on the phone, but that was nearly impossible. He offered comfort, he asked questions, made suggestions and encouraged us to do what we could. Otherwise, we were completely on our own, all the way.

As hard as it was to not hold resentment over our privation, Will's council to us was much like the words found in Romans 12:19. (The Message, paraphrased)

"Don't insist on getting even; that's not for you to do. "
"I'll do the judging", says God. "I'll take care of it."

We were taken advantage of, but it was not in Will's nature to hold a bitterness in his heart. Over the phone and many times afterward, he reminded us that this was a minor setback in the big picture and God was in control

Grabbing The Brass Ring

Surprisingly, it did not occur to me to pack up the kids and *run* back to California. I don't think the kids felt like running either. We just pushed up our sleeves and went to work.

This was to be our home in just a few short weeks. This house, once Will's home was now in a state of near destruction. Clearly living in the house was not an option at this point. Now, we were 'homeless', in a sense.

The nights were getting quite cold by now. But, after considering our alternatives, we all agreed, quite eagerly, to live in our camper while we tackled the house. There we could be ourselves in a warm, clean and friendly enviornment.

We faced a discouraging situation, but the kids grabbed the brass ring and joined me in going another round.

It was challenging, but together we faced it with sheer determination. After having the house fumigated, we armed ourselves with a wheel barrow and snow shovels. We began clearing out the debris making little escapes from the overpowering stench for a momentary breath of fresh air. As I think back to the time, I feel such pride in how Mike so cheerfully and willingly took over the job of masterminding reconstruction. Lorna and Lisa had been through the process of cleaning up this house once before and knew exactly what to do. Chris, age 7 now, helped out in different capacities. What an amazing crew! What a family!

Quick trips to town for new supplies of disinfectant, cleaners, scrub brushes, and mops, we began seeing possibilities of this becoming a home again. Amidst frustrated tears and outbursts of laughter, teasing and making jokes, more burn piles and lots of elbow grease, we had accomplished what we'd set out to do. Our mission was accomplished. The work was done. The house was ready. We could go home.

Snow had come that evening before our departure. But we were so eager to be going to our home in California and to Will's comforting arms, we remained undaunted.

It was Halloween and we agreed that after the grueling work we'd just done, we needed a bit of fun. Before leaving town, Mike drove us into Aberdeen so the girls could take Chris trick-or-treating. Mike and I followed along in the pickup while the others merrily ran from house to house filling their bags.

We came to a lovely large Victorian house with a wrap-around veranda on one corner. On approaching, they could hear very strange screechy sounds coming from the high bushes that surrounded it. Chris, only 7, wasn't too sure he wanted to do this one, but both girls coaxed him. Gathering all his courage, he clung to his older sisters and knocked on the door. Bravely waiting until the door v-e-r-y slowly, squeaked open….. a large black spider dropped in front of their faces. They were greeted by an ugly cackling witch. Right behind her came a bald creature with one eyeball hanging down over one cheek. Without hesitation, Chris turned and took a flying leap over the railing and bushes, shrieking, "EeeAaahhh!!" at the top of his lungs. Landing on his feet he did not stop running until he jumped, pale and panting, into the safety of the pickup.

◦

What joy to arrive home to Palo Alto again and feel the warmth of our family home and a hot dinner that Will had prepared.

Will had promised a trip to Disneyland before we left California if we could get all the preparation for our move done in time. This was the proverbial 'carrot and the stick' technique that put everyone eagerly to work. And, let me add, with so much accomplished, it was a reward well deserved. We were a family who could work hard together in the worst conditions, play together in the best and proud of who we were!

With the new day ahead of us, and multiple tasks awaiting, we began serious packing. Boxes began piling up in every room, each marked with the contents or who it belonged to.

The biggest task we faced was painting the exterior of the house. After picking out the paint and gathering the tools, we proceeded. This was a hard job, and everyone took their turn cheerfully, knowing when the job was finished, we would be taking one last trip to Southern California and Disneyland. In two weeks time, all was finished. The camper was ready and we headed south. Everyone was filled with anticipation of the breathtaking rides and experiences that awaited us. Chris was only 5 months old when we were there last and did not remember. Seeing it through the eyes of a seven year old, made it new all over again for the rest of us.

❧

The day came for our big move and the largest U-haul truck and a large U-haul trailer arrived. A crew of Mike's friends and Will began loading them as well as packing the El Camino, the pickup and the car to the limit, leaving only enough room for passengers. Neighbors and friends stopped by to pay their 'well wishes' and say their 'goodbyes.' By late afternoon, we were loaded and ready to take off.

It was not the wisest thing to begin this journey when we all were so tired, but we had agreed we would drive only as long as we could. We had not taken into account the difficulty of finding a place for our caravan to easily pull into. The hard part came when the sun set and we now traveled against the glaring lights of on coming traffic. I was driving the El Camino. So sleepy, I know there were miles that I could not account for. Hours later, stretched beyond our limit, we stopped for a good night's sleep.

As we crossed the miles through Nevada into Idaho, we grew more and more eager to get to our new home. Our minds were full of plans. I pictured each piece of furniture in its proper place. Will visualized how he would turn the old barn into a cabinet shop. Each one of us had our dreams for this new life ahead of us.

The warm sun was still high in the sky, it was a beautiful fall day as our entourage drove through Aberdeen. Only seven more miles to go! At last we pulled into the yard. The ignitions were turned off and engines went silent. We stepped out to breath in the fresh country air. Flocks of birds sat in the tall trees, chirping their welcome. We listened, drinking in the quietness around us.

Only a short time left before the sun would go down on our first day. Will raised the big door to the U haul truck and he and Mike began removing the beds to carry into the house and set up. We would unload the rest the next day.

Our First Idaho Winter

Two weeks after we arrived, the weather changed and it began to snow. What a shock to this family, coming from sunny California where temperatures rarely drop below 50 degrees. At the same time, we discovered a repulsive smell coming from the basement. The ancient metal septic tank that we had planned to replace in the spring had rusted through. I was in a panic. Our friends would arrive in just one week for Thanksgiving and we had just been thrown back into primitive days! It was back to the outhouse for us! I was desperate to make sure we had toilets working by then.

Immediate measures were taken to hire a back hoe to dig a drain field and hole for a new tank. Will and Mike braved the bitter snow and low freezing temperatures, but in record time, we had a new system installed.

The winter snows continued to pile up. Our first winter! Heavy clothing, boots, bed clothes, electric blankets and oil stoves, non seemed to warm the bitter cold that penetrated our bodies to the bone. The vicious winds that caught the plastic weather guard on the windows sounded like it was tearing at the house, made it feel colder still.

This was our introduction to life in Idaho.

Months before we moved, it had already been decided to restore and convert the 70-year-old rock barn into a cabinet shop. This barn had set idle for many years. In these horrid weather conditions and throughout our first bitter winter, Will and Mike tore down walls and broke up stalls. Using the little Ford tractor, they scraped and removed decades of accumulated dirt, rocks and manure from the building. They smoothed out the floor, laid gravel and conduit for electricity and finally a concrete floor.

Once they had electricity to light the place and work tables built, the barn was transformed into a clean environment for production. With photos of our kitchen and bathroom remodel from our home in California, and with the confidence of a few people, requests for work began coming in.

We designed our own logo *Lazy Y Custom Cabinets*, named for the Harder's registered cattle brand. Along with attending to required legalities, we had invoices and business cards printed up, purchased some more equipment and we were in business.

Many trips were made to the city for supplies, over the snowy roads throughout these bitter months . We soon learned that was a way of life for those of us who lived in the rural area.

Aberdeen Idaho was Will's home town, but for the rest of us, moving there presented a new challenge. Coming from the city, we found priorities and methods of doing things very different from ours.

The winter storms began to wane. The spring thaw was a welcome sight and soon green began to peek through and buds formed on the trees. Spring was near.

City Folks On The Farm

In California we had an automatic sprinkler system that daily watered our beautifully landscaped yard, keeping it looking lush and lovely. Here, they flooded their lawns with water from an irrigation ditch once a week until it was ankle deep and the grass lay flat for two days after. Only the larger farmers had advanced sprinkler systems and that mostly for their crops, while the smaller farmer, like us, still irrigated from a canal that branched out into many small ditches and had to be maintained by hand and shovel.

One of the big frustrations of irrigating like that is the pesky gophers who dug up from their underground tunnels to the surface. This caused all the water that was purposed to flow down the corrugates between rows to disappear into the tunnels, robbing the vegetation of the water it needed to thrive. It was a constant battle for the one who tended the field, walking for miles and covering up the holes with their shovel, only to return the next day to find more holes. Traps were used and occasionally the gophers served as good target practice as well.

A main canal ran through the county, connecting to smaller ditches, supplying water to the farmers at intervals where it branched off to service individual fields. This main canal was wide and quite deep. It ran through our property and Will remembers what fun it was, when he was growing up, after a long hot day, to go down to the canal, going skinny dipping in the moonlight, surrounded by the serenade of millions of frogs. This wouldn't have been a bad alternative to the private swimming club with its beautiful pool we had enjoyed in the city--if you didn't count the mud bottom and the leaches...and the mosquitoes. Sadly, however, this was no longer an option for a summer swim. Through the technical progress of modern agriculture, the chemicals now used for crops filtered into the water, and it was no longer safe to swim in. Not a great loss in my way of thinking except that it consequently killed the frogs, silencing their joyful song.

We were accustomed to city life, where everything we needed was within walking distance or a short drive. In Aberdeen, we were able to buy groceries and do a bit of emergency shopping locally, otherwise we drove 50 miles to Pocatello for major shopping. This took planning ahead.

If you needed to make a quick trip into town to do some business during your lunch hour, forget it. There is an old saying about country towns, "They roll up the sidewalks at noon." In Aberdeen that tended to hold true. Some businesses would be closed from 12:00 to whenever they happened to return. Still as the farming industry progressed that began to change.

❧

It takes a lot of grit to take city kids and teach them how to work the fields. Especially if you've been in the city yourself for 30 years. Not only is this a totally new task for them, they aren't use to the heat, mosquitoes and tedious labor, and farming in the past 30 years had changed.

Mike was enlisted to irrigate the crops. Turning a 'green' city boy into a farmer is a challenging task. Just imagine him battling the gophers who were digging holes where he was trying to make water run up and down a mile of corrugates! You can understand he may be thinking of running back to the city.

Then his sisters and I were also sent to the field to hoe and thin sugar beets. This is not what we had signed up for. To his disappointment, Will found we didn't work fast enough so he ended up hiring this done as well.

But, oh, there was much more to learn that summer! We had only just begun.

Living Off The Land

In the country you can't just run to the corner store for a gallon of milk. Will had the perfect solution. Squeeze it yourself! This remedy, he assured us, netted numerous benefits. Fresh milk, thick cream every day, and homemade butter. Mmmmm! Nothing like it! Yes, indeed. What we needed now, was a cow!

The city kids were indoctrinated in the virtues of rising before the sun, filling their lungs with the fragrant country air as they performed their cow doodies~I mean duties. Wouldn't that be splendid?

In reality, the routine required donning rubber boots and winter coat against freezing temperatures and driving snow to drive half a mile to the neighbor's barn.

Convincing Bessie to cooperate for her morning extractions was a minimum two-city-kid task. It required treading mud while fighting the lashing wind, cornering the wild-eyed creature while speaking in soothing tones (when you really wanted to scream bloody murder) until you could attach the lead rope and lure her one-ton little self into the milk barn. It helped of course to assure her that this was, after all, for her own good. It was for us all. So we were told.

We did enjoy the fresh milk and the novelty of homemade butter, of course. But only when the cow didn't step in the milk bucket, doing her "mad cow dance", just after stepping into her own cow pie before you were done. Needless to say, the fresh milk idea got stale pretty quick. Eventually Bessie was sold and we returned to the grocery store.

Even gardening was different. Who would've thought? I enjoyed raising a small garden in California, so when spring came, I was eager to do the same in Idaho. I wanted a place close to the house where I could step out in the morning to look at it, talk to it, water it and putter for a minute or two.

But, Will had a different view of what my garden should be. After all we would be raising much of our food from it, as his mother had in years gone by. Remember all the out dated jars of green beans we'd thrown out? So he plowed a small *field* for me out behind the barn near a high ditch of water. To top it off, he finished the ground by plowing corrugates, which in simple terms, were long rows of small hills about 2 feet apart.

When he eagerly called me to see his handy work, I just stood there stunned. This *field* was my *'little'* garden? And what were all the 'little hills' for? I was speechless. But only for a moment, before I began to wail with dismay and frustration at the immense size of the thing.

Questions and more questions tumbled out of me,

How was I ever going to water it? In California, a single oscillating sprinkler had done the trick. Here we had only one outside faucet. How could one hose and a sprinkler reach to all this space? Will assured me that we were in Idaho now, and he would teach me the 'Idaho way'. I learned that after you planted your seeds on top of each hill, the water came trickling out of the big ditch and you had to direct it with a shovel down the long rows until it reached the other end, only to redirect it for the next row…pretty much an all day job. That's if there were no gophers to sabotage your efforts.

But I already knew how to raise a garden. I knew the joy of going out to water it, tend it, watch it grow. It was never this difficult in California. Right then and there, I seriously considered the idea of running back! It would not be the last time I thought about it either. My grandiose ideas of my happy little farm life began to disintegrate.

I had convinced Will that I understood the concept of raising a few vegetables and flowers. So he left me and the younger children to prove ourselves while he proceeded to tend much larger crops.

But very soon we were completely overwhelmed by the extreme heat, and the volume of weeds combined with the impossibility of making water run up hill. The swarms of pesky mosquitoes which I was allergic to, covered us from head to toe whenever we stepped outside or worked in the garden. They were so bad, no amount of bug spray could deter them. If you opened your mouth, they would fly right in.

The next thing I learned was that weeds grew faster in Idaho than anywhere else in the world. And they were not just small weeds. They would develop into stalks the circumference of a young sapling right before your eyes, if not nipped in the bud. I was to learn that weeds grew not only on the small hills, but also in the little 'valley's' of the corrugates. There was no keeping up with them. Old seeds begat more seeds. Even the poor little vegetable and flower seeds we tried to nurture were inundated by the bullying weeds and refused to thrive.

This was definitely nothing like gardening in California! Countless other things demanded our attention beside the garden. Eventually, I decided "no more garden." The weeds won. This of course did not win me any admiration from my husband. But, eventually, I would make that up to him. I had no doubt. I had my ways.

I was trying to acclimate to the task of keeping house that had shabby floors with no carpeting, taking laundry from the second floor to the basement, and hanging it outside. Plus, fixing 3 meals a day, which I was not use to. In California, the children were happy with a snack at lunch if they were home and Will was at work. I didn't take into consideration that the country air also stimulates a ravenous appetite.

There just never seemed enough time for everything.

Will and I had always enjoyed working together on projects, so in theory, that was the plan for our farming adventure. But before I knew it, and probably for all practical reasons, "*we*" became a term used to delegate work in my direction. At least that's how it seemed. Take for instance, the idea that "*we*" would raise all our own food. "*We*" would raise chickens for eggs and meat supply. He calculated that if "*we*" froze enough chickens for 2 dinners a week for a year, "*we*" would need around 200 baby chicks. I was not altogether foreign to raising chickens, but this amount seemed overwhelming to me.. As long as I can remember, my mother raised chickens. Although I had little to do with it growing up, I was familiar with the process. I'd always hated the smell of grown chickens, but I had fond memories of how cute and sweet smelling the babies were. If my mom could do it, I surmised, so could I.

My mother was successful in raising White Rock chickens, so it seemed reasonable to call her and get information from her about breed, care and the proper feed to start them on. After all, she knew everything there was to know about chickens….accept for 'Idaho chickens.' Someone recommended a breed that did best in Idaho. "What difference did the location make?" I questioned. "A chicken is a chicken." But Will insisted we order the recommended breed…..all 200 of them!

I knew mom was always careful to purify the water by adding special pellets to keep them healthy, and I was adamant we had to do the same. But, no one seemed to know what I was talking about and could not supply anything of the sort. We were directed to use a special feed where *everything* was included to raise healthy chickens and there was no need for supplements. This did not sound right to me, but what did I know about raising 'Idaho' chickens?

The first week our new babies arrived, we had an April snow storm and the little place we had for them was not warm enough. So in the middle of the night, Will and I had to trudge through the snow and create a hood heated by our little camp stove for them to hover under. Rest assured, we never used that stove for camping again!

I kept in close touch with my mom. I cried in her ear on the phone, worried when they began looking puny while some dropped over dead. So my mom sent me some purifying tablets of her own to put into the water. But by this time, the few chicks that had survived had feathers and were getting as big as turkeys! It was too late, the damage had been done and they were too sick to fully recover.

Will opened the pen to give them fresher air and to let them roam, hoping that would help. But this gave them too much freedom, which left poops on our front door steps or wherever they happened to be. This was one thing I just could not tolerate! And when they began roosting in the trees at night, we knew we'd lost complete control of the matter. I was not sure how this would work out. This project was not going well!

Mike's California friends came for another visit on their motorcycles and one had his dog with him. We didn't give much thought, until the following morning Will looked out of the bedroom window to see white mutilated chickens dotted all around the yard! While we had been sleeping, the dog had himself a spree. Will was horrified, while secretly I was ever so delighted, for now there were less to butcher. The few survivors turned out to be too big, too tough to eat, even after cooking in a crock pot for hours. It turned out much like elephant stew that no one could eat. The rest went to the dumpster. No more chickens…ever.

Adventures On Horseback

Our girls had dreamed of having horses. The first summer we were able to board a mare and her colt so they could get used to the demands of having a horse. We didn't have a proper saddle, only a little "pancake saddle" consisting of a cushion with stirrups and a single strap.

One day, Lisa rode double with a friend while Lorna followed on another borrowed horse. All seemed leisurely enough until they turned and headed back toward the barn—and Momma Mare's little baby! They weren't prepared for the jolting action of the high-speed trot and bounced violently atop the now loose pancake of a saddle. Despite their best efforts the crazed momma was not going to slow down for anyone. The strap on the cushion worked its way loose and Lorna watched helplessly as the two girls slid as one unit like an avalanche right off the horse's back.

They landed in a screaming heap on the rough cut stubble below. The friend landed on her arm, snapping her wrist and the spooked horse ran off ~ in the wrong direction.   Lorna stayed with the injured girl while Lisa went after the horse. Traipsing across harvested grain fields and sagebrush wasteland, she finally caught up with the creature in the neighbor's yard a half mile away.

It was dusk by now, the horse was wild-eyed and visibly spooked. Lisa was able to corner the animal and grabbed its bridle, which the horse did not appreciate. It reared up on its hind legs, raising its forelegs up in violent protest. The horse's knee clopped Lisa right in the jaw, knocking her out.

Fortunately, the neighbor was home. Hearing the commotion, he ran out into the yard and found Lisa laying unconscious in a puddle of mud. By now, it was almost dark. Mistaking the mud for blood, he panicked. He called us immediately, and we headed over to his house, calling ahead to the volunteer ambulance service to meet us in town. It was terrifying to see her lay there unmoving. We carefully gathered Lisa's limp body out of the mud and laid her in the back seat, wrapping her in a blanket. Next thing we knew, she was in the ambulance heading toward the nearest hospital 20 miles away, Will and I following behind. The other girl followed close behind in another car with her family.

We all waited anxiously for the doctor to come talk to us, but he never came. Worried she might have very serious injuries, we finally found someone to look for him. Only to learn he had admitted Lisa and gone home without bothering to speak to us. She had steadily regained full consciousness and was placed in a joint room with her friend who had broken her arm.

Both were released the next morning. It wasn't until we arrived home and removed the bandage from the injury on her jaw that we discovered the medical team had not even bothered to clean all the mud from the wound! Guess that's how they do it in the country! Thereafter, we avoided that

204

hospital and referred to it as the "stopping off placed to the morgue."

We got better saddles after that, and better horses. Which helped, but it didn't prevent further injury. Lisa found herself being bucked off again, into a big rock pile that left her bruised in numerous places.

On another occasion, Lisa watched, terrified, while Lorna fell from her running horse, one foot still caught in a stirrup! The massive animal was determined to get home for some oats and nothing was going to stop it! Annoyed that the drag of Lorna's body was slowing it down, the horse began to kick and buck. through the rocky dirt and stubble, the horse ignored her screams and ran. Fortunately, Lorna was able to break herself loose, suffering only minor cuts and bruises. It was the trauma of this experience that haunted her for years to come.

◈

Will and I took the horses out on one occasion. Our first and last occasion.

An attraction to our place in the country was the vast pasture land in the "back 40." This area was located about a mile from the American Falls Reservoir and largely composed of swamp land. Because of the water level, it remained green for many months of the year, making it ideal for grazing cattle. There were small cliffs and rocks out there and the green, lush grass, manicured by the grazing was our very own private sanctuary. We often took a couple of sandwiches in our knap sack and walked out there to sit on a cliff, looking out over the lake with the mountains in the background. It was a peaceful place to sit and reflect and dream. In the fall season it was a prime place to hunt ducks and pheasants.

It had been many years since Will or I had been on a horse, but we felt brave enough to try it. All went well for a while until Will's horse stumbled and spooked, throwing him off onto a pile of rocks. By the time we got back home, his pain had grown more intense and he was developing a large contusion under his left rib. This called for a trip to the doctor in Pocatello. By now, everyone's enthusiasm of having horses was beginning to dampen rapidly.

Out of the Swamp

Meanwhile, "back at the ranch," Mike had been entertaining his best friend and his girl friend who were visiting from California. He wanted to offer a bit of adventure to his city friends and show off the sights of our small kingdom. Still having a hefty dose of "city spirit" in him, Mike had a great idea.

He grabbed a 6 pack of beer and together, they rode the little Ford tractor that Will grew up with, out to the swamps in the 'back 40.' Actually, they rode it right *into* the swamp. Needless to say, they got stuck. The more they tried to free the tractor the deeper they dug themselves into the bog. The day was getting hot and all this hard work was making them very thirsty. Fortunately, they had the six-pack! Refreshed, they worked even harder, only to find the tractor sinking deeper.

This was beginning to look serious! Then, they hit on a brilliant idea! They went to the neighbors and borrowed a bigger tractor.....and promptly drove the big tractor to the swamp. Aah...yup, right *into* the swamp, too! This calls to mind the adage, "If at first you don't succeed..."

By the time we arrived home it was almost supper time. Mike and his friends had given up on the tractor idea and had just returned to the house on foot with the idea in mind to get the pickup.

As they relayed their story, Will's jaw dropped and his eyes popped. *Now they wanted to drive his pickup into the swamp, too?* He cleared his throat and braced himself. Putting aside the pain in his side, we all jumped into the truck and were off to the back pasture to see what plight our kids had gotten into. We were stunned to see that the huge tractor tires were sunk to the axels.

By now it was evening so there was nothing left but to wait until morning. There was a constrained air around the dinner table that night. Little was spoken.

In the light of a new day, the mood had settled. The whole family drove out to the swamp, hoping something miraculous had happened overnight. Oddly, the stress had diminished, there was work to be done. As we all focused on the task at hand, it became a light-hearted day. Everyone began carrying large lava rocks to pack around the tractor wheels, in hopes that would give the leverage they needed.

When the owner of the big tractor came walking over the hill to see *his* tractor buried to its axels in the swamp, the situation became somewhat sobering again. He stood there numbly for a while. Silent. Then, seeing there was really nothing he could do, he just quietly sat down and watched without a word. He was a man of 70 years, a good friend and neighbor and it was an embarrassing situation.

The guys continued to work well into the afternoon with chains and poles, planks and the rocks we girls carried in ~ whatever they thought might possibly do the job. Everything just seemed to sink into the bottomless quagmire of the marsh and every effort to move either machine only buried them deeper. Exhausted and depleted of ideas, we were heartened to hear a deep rumbling noise approaching us.

We looked up to see a much larger tractor coming toward us, rising up over the sage-covered hill like a 530 horsepower cavalry! Another neighbor had heard of our predicament and came to the rescue with a long chain and a winch. He approached the tractors from the *other* direction and with minimal effort, both were set free.

That's another thing that is different about the way things are done in the country. When you get in a bind, the neighbors will lay aside their own agenda and come to your aid.

The Master Carpenter

Before we left California, Will had developed his skills in woodworking by building a few basic cabinets as needed here and there over the past few years. Before we sold our home, we wanted to do an upgrade. He had in mind to just build new flat doors, but I had been observing kitchens for a while already. So I took him to see commercially-built cabinets displayed in the stores. "This is what I really want." I said. " Do you think you could build that?"

After some careful examination, he said "I would have to have special equipment to do it like that." He loved this kind of challenge, besides he wanted to please me. He began calculating the cost of materials as well as the equipment needed. After he purchased a few pieces of equipment he proceeded to remodel the kitchen and the bathrooms in our Palo Alto house.

Friends and prospective buyers who saw the final result raved about the beautiful custom cabinets, giving Will the inspiration to take this skill to Idaho and begin a cabinet-making business.

୶

Will was never satisfied until he had given his best. He was always ready to learn and stretch his knowledge, to raise the bar for himself as well as for others. Because people admired the craftsmanship and integrity of his work, our customers began sending others to us.

Soon we had all the work we could handle. For a time, Will hired a man to help.

When Will learned that Idaho State University was taking bids on 150 chests of drawers for the dormitories, he did some research and won the bid. We were excited for this good-sized job. It would be all assembly work, so the task seemed to work smoothly.

The whole family got involved. Will manufactured the cabinets and I sanded and finished them. He and I worked together on the design and sales end of the business. Lorna and Chris often helped with sanding wood panels or clean up.

Mike helped some, but by now he was employed with a well-drilling crew that sometimes took him away from home for two or three days.

Lisa preferred to be in the house, cooking. One of her many talents manifested itself in her ability to create delicious things to eat. After a long day of working in the dust and noise, it was a delight to come in and sit down to the lovely dinner she had prepared.

Whatever Will attempted to do, if he saw a piece of furniture or cabinetry that was unfamiliar to him, he would research the technique used to produce it. He read magazines and books on the subject and talked to experts to become acquainted with the subject. In doing so, he built some lovely pieces of furniture such as a cradle, various styles of china cabinets, glass topped tables, heavy turned posts for furniture pedestals or stair balusters and newel posts. Will built a gun cabinet which he and Mike took to Las Vegas and Salt Lake City to display at gun shows.

Among orders for sometimes the unusual, we received an order from a law firm in Idaho Falls who was taking on a junior partner. We were recruited to build him a desk and credenza. Over time, we built several others for them. However, it has been an honor to know, the first partner became Senator of Idaho and still remains in office. These are only a few of the specialized pieces he crafted.

Putting together the practical hands-on knowledge he already possessed, he taught himself many skills. Some of this interest may have been sparked in his childhood when he helped the carpenter build the addition to his family home. When he was seventeen, he remodeled his own room. This room was an object of his pride.

Cabinet making was not just a job for Will. These cabinets were built to fulfill the desire of his client. With each measure, each cut, each nail driven, he personalized his work by meticulously creating a masterpiece that would please them for years to come. For Will, this was an art.

Will relied greatly on God for his strength, guidance and provision. It occurred to him one day early in his woodworking career that Jesus had been a carpenter here on earth. That gave him a very special connection with Him and he delighted in speaking of it from time to time.

I enjoyed designing furniture and rooms, while Will finalized the elevated drawings to measure, calculating materials needed, cutting and building. Sometimes he questioned how some of my designs would work. I just told him that he was the master builder and I knew he could figure it out. And usually he did.

The sawdust built up and the woodshop filled with wooden boxes that would soon fit into someone's kitchen or bathroom. The boxes needed trimming and sanding and finally finished with a stain and lacquer. That was my job. It was very messy work that needed to be done in front of fans that would draw the highly flammable fumes outside. The fans by themselves were inadequate to protect me from breathing the very strong fumes. Even though I wore the required air mask, in time it began causing respiratory problems.

The work was physically demanding and often required late nights and weekends to meet a deadline. But seeing the final result of our hard labor in someone's home and hearing the appreciation of our clientele was the moment for which we had worked.

Keeping the work coming was always a challenge. As people saw our work in homes they visited and happy customers shared their satisfaction through word of mouth we rarely needed to advertise.

The South Eastern Idaho State Fair was held in Blackfoot during the first week of September. Every year we took our display unit, specially designed for the available space. We showed a model kitchen that featured the strength and endurance of dove-tailed drawers, a seldom-used process in present-day cabinetry. Other features were custom divided drawers, a corner 'appliance garage,' gun cabinets, pantries and more.   Over the 6 years we displayed our work at the fair, we talked to 100's of people, collecting names and addresses. Each person who stopped at our booth was invited to enter our drawing for a sample of our work. We then used their names to follow up in months to come.

Together, Will and I held appointments with potential clients in the evenings. We sat down with them, listened to what they're needs and desires were and proceeded to draw out a plan. . We always enjoyed this time, as we got to know many new people and shared in making their dreams come true. In the process we gained a few life-long friends.

For many years, people from all over Southeast Idaho coveted his cabinets for their homes. Will's work ethics, his meticulous craftsmanship and the dove-tailed drawers rivaled the quality of fine furniture, earning him a strong reputation. People could count on receiving the superior work he promised.

❧

The summers were hot. Like any endeavor, problems arose from time to time. Things didn't go right or we'd hit a slack in work. Those became the times that would stress us.

I know Will sometimes became anxious, although he tried to disguise that by taking long walks alone at night, or inviting me upstairs to kneel before the bed and pray with him. He was the provider. He was the wheel that kept things in motion. We all depended on him. He took this responsibility very seriously and carried his stresses quietly. Still, many times when I felt his tension, mine would intensify. Our stress would feed off each other until, much like a stone rolling uncontrollably down a steep hill, it gathered more and more momentum, and we would lash out at each other. We both regretted those times.

Will worried about meeting deadlines and paying bills, time management and all the many aspects of running a business. For every challenge, Will came up with a solution. When one thing didn't work, he didn't give up, he just found a new way. Although we couldn't always see where the next job was coming from, whenever we finished one job, someone called with another. We were clearly in God's hands and Will never failed to remind us of that.

I found this poem that Will wrote years ago obviously during a time of personal struggle. It shows his wrestling through times of adversity and coming through with an even greater sense of God's faithfulness and love.

> The twisted years of yesterday
> Have shown us now a better way
> In those days I often thought that I would sway
> against the gates of Hell by break of day.
> In other days
> I thought that God was Hell and Fire
> but now
> I think that maybe
> God is Love and truth.
> Even desire
> For a woman and children around my fire
> to share my love
> and my desire.
> ~Wilfred E Harder~

Very often Will would halt everything and whisk me away to spend the night somewhere with him. At times our 'get away' was combine with an appointment with a client outside our own residential area. Other times we might spend the night at Lava Hot Springs. It would give us the opportunity to regroup and start afresh, to relieve the tension and renew our love. Those special dates, were a 'marriage saver' for us.

It was comforting to know that Will had a special connection with God, and I had confidence that Will would always find a way to make things work.

You Can Do Anything

When any of us took on a new task and needed assistance, Will would patiently take us step by step through the process, often learning along with us. He was eager to accomplish things and encouraged others to do the same.

"You can do anything you set your mind to" was his motto. When people admired his handy work, they would often say, "I wish I could do that." And he would tell them, "You can. Anyone can, but it doesn't just happen. Like anything in life, you have to commit to it to make it work."

I was in a woodworking class the year we were in high school at Berean Academy together. A few evenings after school, Will came to the wood shop to help me with my lamp building project. Little did we know at the time, one day we would be building things together for a living or that someday he would be teaching woodshop to middle-school students.

I developed an interest in pottery when the children were little Since money was a pinch I couldn't afford to buy it. I discovered that classes were available where I could learn to make my own pottery. Will encouraged me to follow my interest. The weekly class for adults was held at a local high school in Palo Alto. This was at just the right time of day when Will would be home from working all night and he would watch the small children. Tired as he was, they often played around him while he napped on the lounge in the sun.

Anyone who has ever worked with clay, either comes to love it or hate it. I loved it and looked forward to each class.

After some months of this, Will saw that I was permanently hooked. Since this interfered somewhat in his getting enough rest, he bought all the equipment for me so I could work at home. I missed the interaction of the class, but this gave a new aspect to my interest as I involved the children. I taught them how to make clay sculptures and how to turn clay on the potter's wheel. They, too, grew to love this new outlet of creativity.

Will felt that a job required the best tools in order to do your best work. He loved tools and sought to have the ones he needed. He always provided me with the best tools for my work, as well.

Everyone in our family eventually became knowledgeable about wood under their father's direction. They learned how to use the power tools and the other processes involved. It became somewhat of a family tradition to create hand made things for Christmas or other gift-giving occasions.

I remember a particular Christmas when each one of us had a little project going in our own corner of the shop, sometimes needing to work shifts so no one would discover our secret. I seem to recall that for one or two dedicated crafters, the lights were still burning as the Christmas morning glow began to light the sky. With the final stages of a project being the spray-on finish, the gifts were often wrapped while still damp and proudly placed under the tree just at dawn. We sometimes laugh when we recall the pungent telltale aroma of fresh lacquer that permeated the room as we came together for the unveiling.

I still have the lovely treasure box Lorna made for me that year. Designed with raised panels that her father taught her to make. That same year, she built an enlarged set of Domino's for him out of oak, as well as the box to hold them. Those will remain as a family heirloom.

When Lisa was expecting her first baby, she and Matt came from their home in Alaska for a visit. Matt and Will spent that time together building a changing table and cabinet for the nursery. Another time Will helped Lisa built a spice rack for her kitchen.

Some of Will's greatest joys was working with his children, teaching them skills, and then seeing the results of their independent work.

As a young boy, Chris and his father built a helicopter and other toys out of wood. One special project was a small racing car, powered by a c02 cartridge for a competition at school. As a youth, he designed and developed artful projects of his own. After he was grown, he had his own cabinet shop for a time. He still carries on his father's woodworking skills, although it is no longer his sole livelihood.

When ever home, At different intervals, whenever Mike wasn't working elsewhere, he worked in the cabinet shop. He found Mary, a beautiful girl from Rhode Island and they married. When their baby daughter, Heather, was born, Mike became a vital part of the cabinet business. This seemed to get into his blood, for he continues his work in a cabinet shop in Ketchum, Idaho.

Both our sons learned the art of woodworking beside their father and became accomplished craftsmen in their own right. The talent and inspiration for meticulous craftsmanship that Will passed on to them reflects in their own homes and businesses.

Miracles

Over the years of raising a family, we are made aware just how merciful was our God. Day by day, even when we are not conscious of them, he performs miracles all around us.

Mike had worked in well-drilling for some time and had a vacation planned. He and a friend were taking a motorcycle tour of the Southwest. On the day they left, I asked Mike if I could read something to him. "Sure" he said.

I read him the 91st Psalm, where it talks about,

'being safe in the refuge of the Almighty', ' He rescues you from hidden traps, shields you from deadly hazards, and protects you with his outstretched arms. If you stumble his arms will catch you. God promises to give you the best care, be at your side in bad times and give you a long life, if you only get to know and trust him.' (paraphrased. The Message)

When I finished, I told Mike, "this is for you. I love you and God be with you". He nodded his head and said "Thanks, Mom, I'll take that". With a kiss and 'I love you too' he was off.

Two days later, he called us from a hospital in Flagstaff, Arizona. He and his friend, made a signal to turn into a rest stop. The driver of the car behind them was not paying attention and rear ended Mike. He was thrown into the windshield of the car and bounced off into the barrow pit. He wasn't wearing a helmet and his bike was in a twisted wreckage. He was alive! It was a miracle!

Shaken from the news, our first thoughts were, 'Thank you, God, for sparing our sons life!' He sounded good. That was encouraging. He had suffered a concussion but doctors at the hospital were allowing to go home the next day. While we were preparing to leave for Arizona, Mike's friends had already, without hesitation, jumped into their pickup and were off to pick him up along with his friend and the two motorcycles.

Having our son come home after such a traumatic event and seeing the mangled remains for his motorcycle, gave us cause again and again to thank God for his mercies.

After several weeks of recovery, Mike became a major part of construction in the cabinet shop, along side of his father. After he and Mary were married and Heather was in the first grade, he moved his family to Ketchum, Idaho to continue in the same kind of work.

Some years later, Chris and his fiancé, at the time, took a trip to Montana over Thanksgiving. We were expecting them home that evening. It was getting quite late and we hadn't heard from them. I was awakened just before midnight. Aware they were not yet home, I was prompted to pray for them. Within the hour, Chris called from the hospital in Blackfoot, Idaho. They had been in a rollover. Shaken from the news, we got up and left immediately.

They were alright, but his fiancé had a slight concussion and they were picking glass out of her hair. Our hearts were pounding from the news as we thanked God for sparing our children. While He was protecting my kids, He woke me to intercede for them at the very moment this happened.

The impact of this event hit us with intense force when we saw his pickup. Thankfully, they were on the road alone when they hit black ice. The pickup rolled several times, crushing the ceiling of the cab down between them. Only a miracle....only God's hand and his band of angels prevented them from being killed!

Should you ask me if I believe in God's miracles, I would tell you, "yes. Without a doubt." Time after time His mercies have been proven.

When a saw blade broke and flew into Will's forehead, cutting a gash to the bone; when Mike was knocked off a motor boat next to the propeller; when our little granddaughter Heather frantically swam out to rescue her dog and couldn't make it back without her daddies help; when I was broad-sided, spun around and rolled over; and in the early years when 'bullish' horses endangered our girls. These are just a few of the amazing reasons we are aware that God has rescued us from serious harm.

"Because he loves me." says the LORD. "I will rescue
him:
I will protect him, for he acknowledges my name.
He will call upon me, and I will answer him:
I will be with him in trouble, I will deliver him and honor
him.
With long life will I satisfy him and show him my
salvation."
Ps 91:14-16 NIV

This old house

The windows were drafty and many crevices were not sealed tightly and dust filtered through. Areas remained unfinished, floors were nearly all wide planks. Then there was the worn out, torn linoleum in the main rooms downstairs. Old cabinets in the kitchen where mice could come and go. Bee's had built their nest and left a huge yellow wax stain on a wall upstairs.. This is where we attempted to make our home.

The old ram-shackled building with animal skeletons in the orchard turned out to be a great house of horrors at Halloween. The old 'out house' near by and a small shed turned into a 'head house'. Dracula had a grave that he popped out of, and the witch lured her victims into her coven by moon light. Best of all, a friend chewed on raw... yes *raw* liver all evening as he sat in an old tin tub filled with cooked noodles!

Our family worked for days on this project. Will took a whole week off from work to help turn the entire orchard into a spook alley. For two or three years in a row, perhaps a hundred people from our community and Pocatello and Aberdeen church groups came. Visitors delighted in this shabby environment, complete with the witches tour through the creepy spook alley and ending with hot cider and a bowl of chili in the house.

⊙

We had been use to a nice home in California, so it was hard for me to entertain guests in this setting.

It had been my hope to get this renovation started right away. We drew out our plans, but Will, being the practical thinker, believed it was wisest to get our business going before we attempted that undertaking. It was hard for me to wait. Keeping up a shabby house was a huge challenge. Very discouraging and time-consuming and things never seemed to appear clean.

Will heard about a local contractor who came highly recommended. Thinking he could be a source for cabinet work, we went to see him at his home. The same house, incidentally, with the wrap around veranda that Chris and the girls visited on that 'scary' Halloween night a few years earlier.

On that visit, we found so much in common with Norv and his wife, Arlene. We began to form a very close bond with his family that has grown stronger over the years. Their children were of the same age as our girls and for years to come we found endless things to do together.

In our third year on the farm, we took our plans to him and he began work.

Will's original room that he remodeled the winter he was 16, was the only one that did not require a major do over. It was a lovely room and an object of his pride. Everything else needed major work.

One of the first tasks was to expose an 8-foot-wide, floor-to-ceiling section of our living room to the outside. Furniture was moved out or covered with sheets, piles of

224

building material and lava rock covered the living room floor, ready for constructing the fireplace. Even though the opening was exposed during the day, a tarp covered it for the night hours.

One particular evening, Will had already gone to bed. The kids and I were watching TV , sitting on new rolls of carpet waiting to be installed on the living room floor. Suddenly a dark creature began darting and fluttering around the room, taking dives in the direction of our heads. Terrified, we covered our heads and screamed for Will to come save us from the bat. Our wails of panic and fear awoke him and he called down, "Coming! Be there in a minute."

Harmless creatures, they say…but not to me. On warm evenings on the farm, the bats would come out. To catch mosquitoes, I was told - only I suspected their main reason was to give me chills! On occasion they would enter the house if they had a secret passage or someone left the door open too long after dark.

The picture that unfolded before our very eyes will be remembered always. Descending down the stairs, v-e-r-y slowly, Will was revealed little by little. First came his big boots….then his bare hairy legs….his bony knees…. thighs….his boxer under- shorts,….then….the best part. A tennis racket gripped in his hands armored with heavy welding gloves (what were *they* doing in the bedroom?)…and finally…. a motorcycle helmet on his head. THE motorcycle helmet. The one I had decorated with green plastic flowers! Thoroughly protected against rabies, he was ready for bat duty!

We were laughing so hard we could hardly breath. While we hid under a table, he skillfully caught the bat and escorted it outside. He became our hero of the 'bat brigade.'

Many years later we began hearing fluttering and scratching in the wall beside our bed upstairs. The bats had somehow created a nest within our walls. It didn't take too long before one by one they began their week-long attack. They would enter through the fireplace in the living room and as quickly as a blink of the eye, they would dart up the stairwell to the bedrooms on the second floor. It was always a challenge to find them because they were masters at finding hiding places and blending in. I was afraid they would get into the closets and hide in the clothes. This called for the return of our hero of the "bat brigade."

We narrowed their entrance down to the fireplace. To keep them contained, Will hung a sheet between the living room and dining room. Every day when he came home from work he would go behind the curtain and collect his trophies. While I stayed in the other room ready to dive for cover, if necessary. The creatures seemed to be multiplying. Sometimes there would be as many as a dozen bats clinging to a curtain or hiding in the crevices of the dark lava fireplace. As soon as he would enter through the curtain they would begin darting wildly around the room. This went on for a week or so until we found their entry point outside along the roofline next to the chimney and sealed it. Will's count was at least 50 bats he had set to freedom during this one invasion. This time, he bravely faced the enemy without the benefit of his bat armor. No tennis racket, no motorcycle helmet, no welding gloves... only sheer grit and raw testosterone!

The bats were not our only incursion over the years; we had other creatures to deal with. I was allergic to bees, so on occasion when I would step on one, my whole leg would swell up above my knee and I was incapacitated for days. I nearly always went barefoot in the house, certainly not expecting to run into a bee. However, it happened.

Then it happened again. And very soon, bees were covering the inside of the windows and collecting amass on the carpet. We checked the outside of the house and again near the roof line by the fireplace we could see them busily coming and going. When evening came and they 'went home' for the night, Will climbed the ladder and filled the opening first with insect spray and then foam sealer. For the most part, this discouraged their entering the house again. It seemed as if Will was fearless. He always looked out for our safety. He was our hero.

Although we would continue to battle various invasions of mice, bugs and bats, (thankfully *no snakes)*, the initial remodeling of this old house went a long way to make our home more comfortable and secure. It consisted of a major make over. Contractors were busy for months, tearing out walls, hanging sheet rock, building a fireplace, an office, laundry room and extra bathrooms. Then there was the painting and carpeting. Meanwhile, Will kept us and an extra hand busy in the shop, building brand new cabinets for our house, while still building for clients as well. In time, we had nearly a new home.

Common Interests

Will traveled the world through the multitude of books he read. Through reading he experienced life with people of every culture, their religious beliefs and their life styles. I would say, his all time fascination was World War II. Not only did it remind him of this time in his childhood, but it encompassed so many other facets of his life. His interest in weapons, history, and service for his country were just some that related in some way.

Will's grandparents came from Germany in the early 1800's and his family carried on the tradition of the native tongue; so much so that he began school in Kansas without knowing a word of English.

During the war he was exposed to German war prisoners that were hired to help his father and neighboring farmers in the fields. Some of them spoke a bit of broken English, so Will was able to communicate a little with them.

Will had a pile of books and magazines for every subject imaginable. Subjects like flying, hunting, guns, science, mechanics, woodworking, were all 'keepers' and *not* to be thrown away. Even without a college education, Will was well read and could easily converse with scholars on many levels.

He was eager to instill the same passion for knowledge he had for learning in his own children. When our oldest was barely beginning school, a World Book Encyclopedia salesman came to our door. Will purchased the entire set immediately. We didn't have computers in those days, where we could google any subject in a click of a key, but he would be prepared for any question his kids would ask. Whenever anyone asked about a word or place he would look it up in the World Book. The children grew up knowing if they asked a question, the first thing Dad would tell them was, "Go get the World Book."

This love for reading gave him inspiration for many applications throughout his lifetime. Once we counted all the "caps" he wore ~ nearly 30. One for every role he played including husband and father.

Often he would tell me in detail what he read, sometimes reading to me, but always eager to communicate what he was learning. I became acquainted with his favorite authors and many of the stories have stuck with me, almost as if I'd read them myself. Many times he had 2 or 3 books in strategic places around the house that he was reading at the same time. I could never figure out how he could keep track of the stories by doing that, but now I often find myself doing the same thing.

Early in our marriage, he considered a number of different career options. Flying for an airline was something he had always wished to do. He took private flying lessons, and found it most enjoyable. He was ready to do his solo flight when we learned we were having our first baby. We did not have health insurance at that time. Knowing this would take extra money he hung up his wings. He always hoped one day to put them on again. Unfortunately, that day never came, but he never lost his fascination of airplanes or interest in flying.

Sharing common interests with his children was Will's greatest delight. Will had helped Mike restore his motorcycles from time to time over the years. Mike bought a vintage 1950 Harley Davidson for a song and gave it to Will for his birthday. What a generous gift from son to father! However, it didn't get used very much, so Mike sold it and purchased a Timber Framing Class for the two of them to take in Port Townsend, Washington. They gathered their wood working tools, loaded Mike's old VW bus and chugged off for the North Pacific Coast on a grand adventure to share in their common interest of structure and building.

Lorna was interested in photography, so when she discovered some used darkroom equipment for sale, she purchased it for her father. Together they screened off a portion of the basement with black plastic that provided them with a dark place to experiment and learn the art of developing their pictures. A few years later, Will taught this skill to students at school.

When Lorna was preparing to go away to college, Will helped her fix up an old VW bug for her transportation. She didn't seemed to mind getting greasy.

❦

From early on, he taught each child caution and respect in handling the guns that were such an important part of his life. He never denied them to see or touch, however he required that each time, they had to ask and follow directions closely. He made it an event. This same respect was instilled in every part of their life.

As Chris grew older, he became his father's hunting and target-shooting partner. They would eagerly look forward to deer hunting season in the fall. You would hear them upstairs on any given evening for weeks, talking as they pounded out reloaded bullets. They made sure they had enough ammunition, took inventory of their supplies, cleaned their guns and collected their food supply and warm clothing. Chris was probably in the 3rd or 4th grade when Will began taking him out of school for the week.

When the first day of open season arrived, they loaded the camper and with all their gear and a few good friends they headed for the mountains. After a week in the woods, they would come home tired and hungry for real food, and Will happily sporting a weeks' growth of beard, but.....no deer. It wasn't the trophy that was so important, it was the hunt and the time away doing the "man thing" together that gave them so much pleasure.

In the summer months, while Chris was still living at home, they would go target shooting or perhaps venture out on a back-packing trip or a camping adventure. In all this time they spent together, Will was able to share his wisdom and build a solid relationship for life. They never seemed to tire of talking about guns. After Chris left home, nearly every phone call they shared and compared their newest discoveries about a certain gun.

When Chris moved to Washington during the late 90s, he purchased an AR15 assault rifle. Will just had to have one like that too. We did not have the money to put down on a gun like that, but seeing how much he desired it, I sold my piano to purchase it. When we went to visit Chris, the two of them took them apart, polished and handled each individual piece as if it were pure gold. Here was father and son, but you could almost imagine two little boys with their heads together intent on the game they were playing.

Will loved to teach the kids new things. There were times he let the little ones sit on his lap and hand him tools when he did leather tooling or other projects

From the beginning, with our own children, later when our grandchildren began to arrive, Will was on the floor, eye to eye with them, every chance he got. He seemed to have a special way of communicating and quickly won them over.

When a new child came to our house for a visit and showed fear of new faces, he brought out the blocks. He got down on the floor and built towers, completely ignoring him until the blocks fell over. Before they knew it, he had them laughing and playing with him.

The little granddaughters loved putting funny hats on Grampa's head and pouring pretend tea for him for their little tea parties. Just ask them; he could 'talk the talk' as good as any tea party guest ever could.

Will delighted in showing the little boys his collection of guns and knives. They loved hearing stories about them and sometimes even got to go out and shoot at tin cans with him.

He built cradles for dolls, benches and a painting easel, but one particular project was a play 'kitchen cabinet' for Heather, our first granddaughter. I stocked it with dishes and pretend food. She was barely 4 when he presented this to her for Christmas. When she saw it, her eyes grew as large a saucers. It was taller than she was and she had to stand on her tip toes as she immediately began examining it.

"Oh, Grampa, thank you, thank you" she eagerly exclaimed repeatedly, wasting no time to begin serving him 'food'. She grabbed a small cloth from one of the drawers and polished the little cabinet from top to bottom, intermittently hugging and kissing her grampa for the wonderful gift. She continued this play long into the afternoon.

Love For Teaching

When the economy took a temporary slump in the mid '80s and work was not coming in as steadily as needed, a friend stopped by to visit. He told Will the local high school was looking for a new woodworking instructor and suggested with his skills he should apply for the position. This sounded most flattering, but Will reminded him he had no college degree. This man, a school board member, thought there could be a way. Will's years in the cabinet making business could be applied to equal college credits, and he could make up the rest through classes while he taught school.

This certainly interested Will, as for so many years he'd desired to return to school to get a degree in teaching or counseling. But. provision for his family came first. With the many debts still to pay, it would be a difficult time financially and now he worried that this venture might prevent him from providing properly for his family.

The rest of us were more optimistic about it than he was. We all saw this to be the opportunity of a lifetime and did everything to persuade him to take the position. Such an opportunity might never come along again.

He was the cautious type and had a way of seeing things more realistic than the rest of us. But we arranged with our creditors to make small payments until we were cleared. In time we saw the results of our efforts and best of all, Will was doing something he'd always had a desire to do.

Arrangements were made for him to move his own equipment to the school, teach his classes, take extra college courses and build cabinets for our own business in the school shop on his own time . This was a major turning point in his life. As long as I can remember, he wanted to have a profession working directly with people and here it was, basically handed to him.

Since knowledge was so high on Will's list of priorities, instilling this skill into the young lives of his students gave him great joy. He loved his work with the students and his colleagues. He earned their respect. The community as a whole came to respect him in a whole new way. We were proud to see him finally getting to do what he had dreamed of nearly his whole life. It took a lot of courage for him to walk into an unknown field without the usual preparation of years of schooling, but Will was always up for a challenge. This one was just another one to which he gave himself fully.

Many hours of his own time were given to his students. It was important to him that each one finish the project he chose to work on. Some of these students didn't always work efficiently and wasted their time in class by making mischief or playing around, and 'Mr. Harder' dealt with them. He always encouraged them and when necessary, used firm discipline.

Discipline was the hardest part, but Will never hesitated to call them into the hall for a stern reprimand or send them to the office. He always contacted the parents to discuss the matter and find a solution to a problem. But in the end of the semester, he was always there to help them complete the task by staying on extra hours of his own time. At those times, I was often recruited to provide soft drinks and homemade cookies for their final marathon. He felt it was more beneficial to the student to make a party out of a difficult task and getting it done, than to give them a zero grade.

While Will taught woodworking, he took computer drawing and technology classes as well as psychology. This certified him for teaching those subjects as well. As part of a technology program he had a dark room installed into the classroom and taught the kids film developing. On occasion he took his students to other schools to compete for structure and weight load of their bridge building models.

He drove the school bus for several years, getting up before daylight to pick up his load of country kids and returning them to their homes after school. Occasionally there were field trips, roller skating trips and other activities that he drove for. He engaged in conversations with his bus students. For special holidays, like Christmas or Valentines day, he had me buy candy bars for him to pass out. His involvement with his students branched into so many avenues as he built a relationship with them.

One evening on returning from his bus route, told me about a 'flying horse' that struck his bus. As he was driving down the highway, out of the corner of his eye, he saw a horse at a distance. Not thinking too much of it, he kept driving, but something caused him to slow way down. The horse had begun to run in his direction, faster and faster until it appeared it was not going to stop. Will was able to stop as the horse came sailing over the fence, landing at neck-break speed on the right front of the grill. Will radioed for help. Of course, this shook Will up a bit, but thankfully, non of the children were hurt, due to Will's for-thought.

But the horse…had to be put down. Later, as a gag, Will was awarded a certificate from the police department for 'catching a flying horse'.

In years to come, former students and parents alike, would speak admirably of him. There were some who came back just to pay a visit to Mr. Harder, one of their favorite teachers.

One former student wrote, "Mr. Harder was a friend and a very special teacher who was always willing to keep looking straight ahead. Anything was possible. I respected him a lot and listened to words of encouragement which has helped with my job and life."

Will would certainly enjoy hearing what people tell me of their children or grandchildren's statements; such as "Hey, yeah, Mr. Harder was 'kick-ass!"

Other memorable comments were from teachers and students: "…a great example to our students". "Mr. Harder always went the extra mile".

Level 1 Reserve Police Officer

It saddened him to know that some of the students repeatedly got into trouble. The ones that especially troubled him were boys without fathers. He was known to invite an individual to go have a hamburger with him after school, just to talk. He cared so deeply for those kids. These same kids, *his kids,* were often on the street late at night. This stirred his heart to show them a better way, that eventually led him to pursue a position with the police department.   Will brought home two big journals about 3 inches thick to learn everything he needed to know about law enforcement and eagerly began to devour every word. He spent a lot of time target shooting at the police range and building up his physic.

By the time he was ready, he went to training camp for a week. At the age of 62, the oldest to complete the stringent training with men years younger than himself, he certified as a Level 1 Reserve Police Officer on the Aberdeen Police Force.

His compassion for young lives had already established a confidence with his students. It was his hope and prayer through this, he would have a positive influence in their lives.

Will gave law enforcement, as well as his teaching, utmost importance. He dedicated himself to both as a ministry. Not only did he live a strong moral example but he never failed to pray for those under his authority as well as for the City of Aberdeen itself. He had taken a sacred oath, vowing to protect, that he took seriously. He was always ready with his duty bag packed, gun loaded and prepared to assist wherever he might be needed, whether within our own city limits, at church, on the road, where ever he went.

In a small town like Aberdeen, things ran fairly routinely. There were the usual commercial doors to check nightly, cruising the streets to keep order, an occasional traffic stop. But a few times he faced real potential danger in dealing with people on drugs. He stood by to keep peace in domestic situations, got bit by a dog, and accompanied his Chief officer in a 100 mile an hour car chase.

One night he was searching for an armed criminal that was reported on the loose and last suspected to be in the warehouse district. Will carefully entered a pitch dark building through an open door, radio on, gun in one hand and flashlight in the other. He was fully alert and ready for what he might face, but, no one was found. Feeling the suspect had to be close, he asked God to deliver the felon into his hands. Will reported later that he felt strongly directed to an old abandon garage a block or so away. Sure enough, the felon was there. When Will called to him to drop his weapon and come out with his hands raised, the man did just that. Once handcuffed and placed securely into the patrol car, Will radioed for back- up.

These two careers were a fulfillment of Will's life long dreams as well as the desire to show compassion to his fellow man with the help of God's spirit within him.

So Who Is Perfect?

Through the stresses of life and the additional pressure that our move to Idaho put into play, the difficulties we faced seemed to overtake us. The fires of adversity can force our impurities to the surface so they can be seen for what they are.

After coming to Idaho and our cabinet business was beginning to take off, we went to a seminar where the minister taught about sacrificial giving. He based his teaching on his own twist on the Biblical principle, "give and it shall be given you." He taught us "the more you give, the more blessings you will receive."

Well, who doesn't want all the blessings we can get? Still new at this 'Christian thing', we began using that principle as we understood it, but it backfired on us. We gave and gave some more, even borrowing to give to 'the church' and forced our creditors to wait…..while we waited for our blessing.

Our minister at the time, supported this, while our creditors were breathing heavily down our neck. It came to a point when Will had to retract a pledge we'd made to the church towards a new organ. He was criticized severely for this action. They said "God would certainly punish you for this". We withdrew from that church; angry with them, and angry with God. For nearly a year we did not attend church anywhere. We just stayed home blaming God and each other.

It began to dawn on us, that we ourselves had been 'sweet talked' into something contrary to God's word. We had been gullible enough to listen to the unsound teaching of a man instead of following our own good sense and checking it out with God.

A quote from a paraphrase, "The Message" in 2 Corinthians 9 says this, regarding giving,

"I want each of you to take plenty of time to think it over, and make up your own mind what you will give. That will protect you against sob stories, and arm-twisting, God loves it when the giver delights in the giving." and it goes on to say, *"God can pour on the blessings in astonishing ways so that you're ready for anything and everything, more than just ready to do what needs to be done."*

We finally realized it was our own fault and quit blaming God. We began the long hard struggle of chipping away at the financial mess we'd made for ourselves. In that process we learned that God was faithful to provide and restore. Even our misguided minds! It's amazing how, over time, by opening our minds and hearts little by little; by developing our trust in him, God can show us areas in our life that he would like to restore to newness.

While we were learning a lot through this process, there were still so many other things for us to learn. More difficulties and stresses, both real and imagined, accumulated, putting pressure on us.

Falling in love is a euphoric experience, one cannot even imagine that the person you're in love with could be anything but perfect. Everything is wonderful and you only see the future as some say, "through rose colored glasses." As lovers, we put on our best face for each other. We want to look our best and put on our best behavior. We communicate our love for each other easily and spontaneously.

Marriage evolves into an intimacy far richer than what you can imagine you will have at the beginning. Because we were so dedicated to each other and determined to keep our relationship beautiful, we resolved to never let our anger go unchecked for long. Making up, acknowledging our wrongs, saying "I'm sorry," always restored us to that special place of tranquility.

However, no matter how deeply in love we were, or how great we were at communicating our love, we were totally uneducated in the art of communication in times of difficulty or disagreements.

Over the years, an ominous cloud subtly caused a great shadow to hover over our relationship and threatened to corrode our peace. We were faced with some painful encounters. We blamed each other for things we should have taken responsibility for ourselves, or took offense of something the other said. It doesn't take long for the list to grow beyond control.

Unexpected hurts and emotions arose, angry words are said. We were totally uneducated in the art of communicating in times of difficulty or disagreements. Through the strenuous years of raising a family and earning a living we let our guard down and almost lost our way.   The little irritations mounted into old unresolved issues. We needed help.

We began attending a small church in Aberdeen. Our young pastor, Dan Pitney, began coming for lunch once a week. It was he who offered to council us. He didn't point fingers, but rather had us list all the things we loved

241

and admired about each other. Then he taught us how to communicate in a non-threatening way. This was a positive beginning, and eventually, we spent 3 years counseling with a psychologist.

We learned so much about ourselves in that time, but this did not solve all our problems either. Things continue to build after the kids had all left home. Everything finally came to a point when Will decided he didn't want to be with me anymore and moved his clothes into a separate bedroom as a first ditch. I was devastated. We were clearly in big trouble. I called our dear pastor friend, Ron. He and his wife, Alberta dropped everything on their schedule and drove four hours to our aid.

They listened to us each tell our side of the story. Then Ron took Will and I aside individually, into another room where he used the principles from a book, "The Bondage Breaker," by Neil Anderson. He counseled us on the importance of forgiveness, having us list everything that had ever caused us pain, forgiven or un-forgiven. Then we made a statement over each hurt on the list, 'In the name of Jesus....(Will/Joan), I forgive you for_____.

It didn't seem like much at the time. But when we came back together after these sessions, Ron told us how important it was for us to express our forgiveness to each other, face to face. What an amazing lightness and joy we both felt as we looked into each others eyes and said, "In the name of Jesus, I forgive you."

This was not the first time Ron had addressed forgiveness. A year or so earlier, I had been wrongly fired from my job with the Senior Citizens Center in Aberdeen. I'd given 6 years of my heart and soul to these people. A select number of them resented my being there, particularly because I was younger and was being paid for my work. They accused me of terrible things in underhanded ways and I was nearly destroyed. Ron suggested at that time, that I forgive them, but my response to him was, "No way! I have no intention of forgiving them. They don't deserve it! I *will not* forgive them"! But he used this same method to talk me into it. "Okay," I finally said. "I'll do it. But it ain't gonna do no good!"

However, the first day after doing this, I came into contact with one of the people who had 'slammed' me. I was amazed to find that I felt *no* animosity! I was shocked! Hey, it did work! It only got easier after that.

Because forgiveness deals with our pain, God commands us to forgive others so that evil cannot take over our emotions. It can destroy us if we allow room for that un-forgiven pain to eat it's way into us. It can rob us of the freedom and joy in our life. That's why Jesus died on the Cross. He gave himself as a sacrifice for the forgiveness of our sins.

God requires us to give up our 'right' to hold anything against another or we suffer the consequences. For Will and myself, the 'sins of blame' had invaded our relationship from time to time to cause near destruction.

Like a boil, un-forgiveness starts to fester and begins to grow until it bursts and spreads it's poison on everything in it's wake.

In taking those vows of forgiveness, we relinquished our 'right' to hold grudges no matter how small.
Our relationship began to grow again. This is not to say that we never disagreed or became angry with each other again, but now we had the right tools to use and our life became richer and our love stronger than ever.

A Christmas to Remember

The winter season can be very unpredictable here in Idaho. This happened to be a year for lots of snow! During the time of Full Moon, we could see such detail for miles, almost as if it were daylight. Sometimes, driving home on the country road to our house, when the moon shined on the crusty snow, Will would turn off the headlights and we would just drive in the brilliant moonlight. It seemed so romantic, much like what our parents experienced as they rode home with horse and buggy late a night ...however, I'd say, we had a definite advantage.

In Southeast Idaho, it's not just the snow, but blowing winds that cause drifts and road closures. Fortunately, our main road was kept open by the county snow plow, most of the time, but on this night, our yard and driveway had drifted full, so we had to park along side and walk in.

It was a beautiful, quiet Christmas Eve scene. The trees heavily laden with fresh, fluffy snow. Massive drifts had mounted right up to our front door with sharp swirls and edges that the wind had sculptured. Inside the colored lights twinkled on the tree and candles glowed.

The full moon shown through the clouds and seemed to light the whole world for miles around while large flakes softly drifted downward. The TV announcer predicted more snow. I sensed the romance of Christmases past. I thought of the fresh outdoor scent of Will coming in from the cold as his winter-chilled arms reached around me. His wet snowy beard and hot kisses covering my face. These were the pictures that danced around in my head as I anticipated the arrival of my husband within the next couple of hours.

It would be just Will and I at home alone this year. The children were all living their lives far away, some out of state, and each of them had plans of their own. Will had volunteered to work the Christmas Eve shift for the Aberdeen Police Department so that others could spend the evening with their children. We would have our own celebration when he got home.

In the time remaining I continued to set the scene for his return. Just that week I'd had surgery on my right shoulder so things took more time than usual, but I'd put together some special food, keeping it quite simple due to my present handicap.

I was deep in my thoughts, anticipating our special evening ahead, as every evening together with Will was special. I clumsily wrestled the table cloth with my free arm, trying to spread it evenly before setting the table with our best crystal, china and candles, when......

I stopped a moment....listening... thinking I'd heard the faint sound of Christmas carols ....but, I reminded myself it was my imagination and continued my one armed wrestle with the table cloth. But, again....I was still hearing the singing.....and it had definitely gotten louder. So loud, in fact, that I dropped the cloth that I had in my hands as I approached the front door, wondering who might chance to come all the way out to the country to sing. Suddenly...

There! Peeking through the side window......familiar laughing faces....my heart stopped. As I threw open the door my heart leaped out of my chest, to see what stood before me......My eyes and mind had not yet caught up with me, but there before me were *all* my children!!

......"but...I thought....you said....how...what" I screamed in delight, I thought my eyes would pop out of my head!

Through the knee deep snow from the road , Mike carried Mary who's leg was in a cast. She carrying a cane, wrapped like a candy cane with red and white striped tape, fastened with a big red bow and looking festive...

"I thought you were in Nevada!" I shouted, excitedly.

Heather, wearing a bright red hat, was holding Lorna's baby Rachel.

Brett was carrying Lorna, nearly 8 months pregnant! Matt and Lisa, too, were among the many faces. Both families had driven over icy, slick roads from different parts of Montana, to get here.

Children peeked around the taller adults, trying to be seen. They all filed in with big hugs and kisses.....and ... suddenly...there was Chris and Rebecca, his bride of one year all the way from Florida! I was stunned. I wasn't sure this could really be happening, or was it just a dream? Just moments before, the room was serenely quiet and suddenly, it was filled to near over flowing with roars of laughter and shouts of joy!

In moments like these, time dissolves into space. It takes a little time for your mind to grasp a hold of reality....and just as suddenly, I realized I'd been caught so unprepared for this glorious invasion.

Since I'd been busily sewing, crafting gifts, and wrapping packages before my surgery, I had just set it all aside and closed the door to my work room which also served for a guest room. All these things zoomed into my mind in a flash. Even as I was beginning to grasp this reality, I suddenly drew in a horrified breath and slapped my hand over my mouth.

Everyone stopped short...what now??? And I said, "Where will I put everyone?"

From the moment the words were spoken, everyone jumped into the act of preparing sleeping space.

The girls went to 'the' room and began packing up my artistic remains and stashing them in places I was yet to find months later. In quick time they had restored the room back to a guest room.

Meanwhile, the men began carrying boxes, one after the other, through the snow across the yard, filled with enough food for a week. Paper supplies, piles of Christmas gifts, suitcases, everything one could imagine.

Rooms were chosen. After joking that there was always the bathtub to make into a bed, Chris and Rebecca chose the 'blow up' bed and placed it in the large upstairs bathroom! That would be their room. Lorna and Brett took the guest room, Lisa and Matt took the hide-a-bed in the living room and Mike and Mary took the twin beds in the pine room. The smallest children were tucked in with parents. The older children spread their sleeping bags around the living room floor where they could keep an eye on the gifts under the lighted tree in hopes of catching Santa filling their stockings that were hung on every knob, nail and hook. Everyone.... yes, everyone had a stocking and by some miracle they were all filled when morning came. But the best part was a short while after the 'big arrival' when Will came home!

As Will approached our home after his night duty, he was puzzled by the cars parked along the road by our drive. He and Lisa had secretly plotted that they would come from Bozeman to surprise me.....but two other cars? He recognized them, yet while he trudged through the deep snow to the house, he still had a feeling that his mind was playing tricks on him. After all, Mike and Mary were on their way to spend Christmas basking in the warm sun in Laughlin, Nevada . They had called on their way just this morning, confirming their plans.

And Lorna was expecting a baby very soon. Besides, they lived in Missoula, Montana and surely, she wouldn't be traveling so far in this storm. He was still rationalizing all this as he stomped the snow off of his boots and entered the front door…….when his face suddenly lit up with surprise and delight to see all those faces!

"Mary, here you are with your broken leg!" and "Lorna, you *are* so pregnant!" he expressed with amazement, "How did you all manage to get through this deep snow?"

He was busy giving big hugs all around, while everyone was holding back their excitement of the *big secret*.

Finally they could contain themselves no longer. Chris, who had been hiding behind the entry wall, stepped out in front of Will. Will's eyes suddenly focused on the buttons of a shirt at his eye level and slowly drifted up into the face of this tall man that stood before him and his head jerked back in shock!

"Chris! You came! I can't believe it!" Will managed to say as he grabbed Chris in a big bear hug and couldn't let go! Laughter, mixed with tears of joy as Rebecca joined the embrace. Our family was complete…..on this Christmas Eve!

During the next few minutes, questions of the how, the what's and the when's were being tossed around and little by little the story behind this wonderful surprise unfolded. Everyone talked at once, wanting to tell their own version.

Chris and Rebecca had planned on coming earlier in the fall, but for reasons unknown to us, they were not able to do that. Mike and Mary had plans of basking in the sun at a resort in Laughlin, Nevada. It would have been lovely for them to come, and we were disappointed for sure, but of course we understood. Little did we know, they had been cooking up this scheme over many phone calls for quite some time now.

So on this night, they risked the snowy skies, the dangers of flying, the harsh weather, slick roads and poor visibility making traveling very difficult. Yet, each of our children were determined to make this a Christmas, we would never forget.

Lorna and Lisa and their families weathered the icy roads from Montana. As they approached the turn off on the highway toward 'home', another car had turned onto the same road from the other direction, just ahead of them. The first car came to a stop at the end of the drive way. It was Mike, Mary and Heather. They had met Chris and Rebecca at the Pocatello airport, when they flew in from Florida, just a short time before. They all stepped out into the snow just as the other two cars pulled in behind them. Like a Christmas miracle they all arrived together.

Here we were, all 18 of us! A dream come true. The small children were too excited to sleep. Eventually, everyone was bedded down for the night and the house grew quiet once again….but only until dawn, when the children's eyes popped open and they scrambled out of their sleeping bags to check their stockings.

"Wake up, wake up" they called to everyone. "It's Christmas morning! Santa came and filled our stocking!"

But, "Santa", who had been up into the wee hours while *he* stealthily moved among the sleeping bodies. Now *he* begged for just a few more winks of sleep, but the children would not hear of it. They jumped and pulled on their covers without mercy, until the adults were no longer able to resist.

Immediately, I went to the kitchen to assume my role as hostess, but before I could even get there, I was firmly apprehended and led to the sofa, informed I was not allowed in the kitchen! They had planned the food, brought all the supplies and had everything under control. How proud I was to stand back and watch my four children and their spouses work together like this.

"Honey, looks like we did a great job with our kids!" I said, smiling at Will. He agreed.

Since the first Christmas with our family, the custom had always been for the youngest to open the first gift and proceed in order of age until everyone had opened a gift. This gave opportunity for each gift to be 'oohed, and aahed' over, and the story behind it told, before starting all over. With so many around the tree on this monumental morning, following this tradition took hours and hours. Once in a while someone would take a quick break to run to the kitchen for a small snack that had been laid out, then eagerly come running back so not to have missed anything.

No one was allowed to 'tear' into a gift without everyone watching. It was considered rude and inconsiderate. Will and I began this 'game', copied from our own family traditions as children and we were delighted to see that our own children carried it on in their own families.

The few days that followed were filled with eating wonderful food, rides on the toboggan being pulled by Grampa's tractor, snowball fights, building the worlds best snowman and coming inside to play a game by the warm fireside.

It was a Christmas for all time. The joy, the laughter and lasting memories of that occasion can not be measured.

❧

This same winter the snow kept piling higher and higher and by January we had 3 feet on the level. Farm equipment was totally covered. A friendly neighbor with a large tractor came to grade out a portion of the yard and with just a tunnel dug from the house to the car gave us access to the outside world.

Will got out his cross country skis and every evening, after he arrived home from school, he took his dog and his rifle and headed across the fields looking for rabbits.

Long past, those days have become precious memories. I still can hear the 'thump thump' as he stomped the snow off of his boots and came in through the back door. I would go to him and get that desired cold bear hug from him and inhale that nostalgic aroma of Jack Frost as his snow soaked beard brushed my face. As he sat down to a nice hot meal, his eyes sparkled with the joy of telling me all that he had seen on his trek.

It looked like such fun and I wanted to try it too. I found it to be more work than it looked like, but doing this with Will was a delight.

Our friends, Ron and Alberta, came for a visit and we rented skies and boots for them. The four of us, dressed in warm clothes from head to toe, made our way gingerly across the field. This was their first time and I was barely more experienced at this than they were, so we stumbled and got our skis crossed up, fell down and got up to try again. Laughter rang across the open space as one or the other of us fell into the pillow of white snow.

At one point, I got so stuck and trying to recover, I only dug down deeper until I was buried up to my hips and laughing too hard to do anything but just sit there. Ron, a true gentleman, turned around to lend me a hand, only for me to pull him down on top of me. We were convulsing in laughter, both too helpless to move.

Right about then, a huge flock of geese flew right over us at low altitude and remembering what geese do best.......we ducked our heads to avoid the 'ammunition' from dropping on our faces. Our laughter escalated until our sides hurt and we had no breath left in us. Alberta and Will were not close enough to help, but eventually we were ready to shed our jackets and we worked our way out. All of us were exhausted. More from laughing than skiing. So, we headed back to the warm fire and a bowl of hot chili.

Joined at the Hip

Through our journey together, through the joys and pain, we found the grace to face the most difficult time of our life. Through our time together, we delighted in each other, developed our dreams and deepen our love.

Something that I valued about Will, was his willingness to be involved in each of our lives. He was always willing to help me when I got stuck in a stressful situation. I, in turn, would help him out as well, and we became a team in so many areas of our lives together.

For every challenge Will came up with a solution. When one thing didn't work, he didn't give up, he just found a new way. I could depend on him to assist with the simple, common courtesies in day to day life. If he was free, he would spring to the task of carrying in groceries from the car, or open a door; help in the kitchen when we had company. If he saw a need, he was ready to help. Countless times, he said to me. "I'll do anything for you. All you have to do is ask."

Being together, doing things together, just sitting quietly or interacting in some conversation or activity, Will and I had this insatiable need to be close, touching. In a crowd, out shopping, taking a walk, it didn't matter where. Invariably you would see our hands magnetically connect with the other.

"Joined at the hip" some people called it, half mocking, half teasing. They perhaps did not understand our soul connection. We adopted that image; claimed it for our own. We were known as 'Will 'n Joan' rolled into one. We did nearly everything together. We sought approval in each others eyes for nearly every situation. Few decisions were made without consulting the other.

Years ago, Will had our names cut out of metal at the fair. They remain on the counter since that time. We would leave little love notes or other important messages under the others name.

Oh, we had different interests. But as a whole we embraced and encouraged those in each other. Will loved the cool summer mornings in Idaho. The clear freshness of the air; often mixed with early morning sound of irrigation sprinklers spritzing the thirsty fields; the morning call of the birds signaling a new day ~ this was his favorite time.

Perhaps his trend to early rising reflects back to the days when he had to get up in the very early hours to go to work in the fields as a youth or from the dusk to dawn hours that he worked in the building maintenance. He often was wakeful at night. Yet, in spite of getting little sleep, he always bounced out of bed in a positive spirit, ready to face the new day. I do believe his connection with God and nature were at their best in these early hours. These were the hours he received his best inspiration and was energized for the day.

I, on the other hand, was a complete opposite. Most mornings I would wake up to the sounds drifting from the shop across the yard. As the first rays of light were cutting a path through the dawn, one might hear saws cutting through a sheet of wood or a power gun shooting nails into pieces of cabinetry he was assembling.

If I woke up before he went out to his shop to begin his work day, I'd be drawn downstairs by the delicious smells of the wonderful hash browns he fixed every morning. He would offer me some, or if he had already eaten, he would sit with me on the sofa and snuggle me for a while. But he always greeted me with a cheery, good morning.. Whenever possible, he would stop what he was doing to hold me in his arms and tell me he loved me. That's what I loved best.

"You should have seen the sunrise this morning. It was so beautiful," he would say. Or "You miss the best part of the day,"

I often wish that I would have enjoyed more of those early hours with him. I know I missed something very precious with him because my inner clock could not function that early.

Certainly, every couple has their unique "love language." One way Will communicated his love to me still replays itself nearly every morning when I get up. The memory lingers as a precious moment in time that confirmed his love and commitment to me. On the days when we could sleep late together or got up at the same time, he would help me make the bed. He would tell me, "I love making the bed with you."

Those precious words resound in my heart and mind forever.

Dreams For Tomorrow

Will was well established in his teaching career, most of our debts were paid and we had more time together. By now the children were all married and gone their own directions. I held a job as a cashier at a local truck stop, and we had a little extra money so we could eat out a bit more often and enjoy more things together. Life was good.

It was 1996. We began dreaming of doing some traveling with an RV. We looked at all the options, compared the cost of the ones we wished for and those we could easily afford. Will and I both loved the fifth-wheel with all the amenities, but knew we would have to get a larger pickup to pull such a load. Or we could go with a smaller, less expensive trailer and use the pickup that we had.

Will found an A-Liner that he was intrigued with. It folded down like a tent trailer, but had a solid exterior. It could be easily towed behind our small pickup and took only a minute or two to set up. It was light and attractive inside. There was room for a port-a-potty. But there was very little floor space. Even though it had a cook top and a sink, I knew I would not be preparing any meals in it.

Will made a deal with me. If I were willing to get this one, we would eat all our main meals out and still have an inexpensive way to do all the traveling we wanted to do.

I agreed.

It was very cozy, in spite of being very small; so small in fact that both of us together could barely stand in the middle. To prevent a major collision, Will would get up first and dress, then go for a walk while I made the bed and dressed. What fun it was to drive along until we needed a little break and could pull over along side of the road, pop up the top and have a snack or take a snooze. We were often approached by curious folks that asked about it and we enjoyed showing them our cute little 'home'.

We were very excited to finally see the beginning of our dream unfold. Since Will was not in school during the summer months, I was allowed to take the summers off from my job so we could spend it together. Our travel plans began in earnest.

◦

I have heard it said, "The brightest light can sometimes cast the darkest shadow."

When we least expected it, a simple routine PSA test changed our lives forever. The results of this test indicated a potential problem for Will. Instead of having an immediate biopsy, he waited a couple of months, simply ignoring the serious potential. It was one week before Christmas when we learned the results of the biopsy were not good.

It came as a complete shock to hear the words 'Cancer.' That dreaded word literally took the wind out of our sails. This cannot be happening to us! Will is too young. We still have so much life to live! We have just begun enjoying our life again. How can it be?

The news came as a big black cloud in our horizon.
We clung to each other in fear and grief…..denying, yet
knowing inside, this was reality.

We notified our loved ones, requesting their prayers. We
researched everything we could find on cancer, collecting
stacks of books from the library, consulted the internet,
talked with people who suggested we seek divine healing.
Some thought we should do alternative medicine and diet.
The doctor told us this particular prostate cancer was very
aggressive and urged for immediate surgery. As the news
spread, the many prayers and love that was extended from
all around the country gave us an enormous amount of
strength and hope.

After prayerfully weighing our options for this most
difficult decision of our lives and looking at it from all
directions, Will and I chose do everything possible. We
changed his diet, consulted naturopaths, sought prayer
and immediately scheduled his surgery the week after
Christmas.

Our number one goal was to preserve our life together
to it's fullest, for as long as God saw fit. In the quiet hours,
our tears blended into our pillow, as we grieved together for
the precious intimacy that was about to be stolen from us,
yet hoping this surgery would magically bring this crisis to
an end, and our lives would go back to normal.

Recovery from the surgery came quickly and Will
returned to school, relying on follow up PSA test results to
ease our fear of cancer recurring. Yet, the emotional ground
shook beneath us as we watched,…and waited…for the
unexpected.

When we began our lives together, so many years
before, we thought we had forever to be together. But
suddenly 'forever' shows the temporal side of itself. Every
day occurrences that once seemed 'earth shaking' begin

to take on less importance. We were in a life and death situation. Each day became more precious just because we had each other '*today.*' *Tomorrows* held no promise. One day at a time. That concept became a force that glued us together for what awaited.

The Gathering Storm

Like a huge wave crashing into a shack built on the sandy shore during a violent storm, news came that Will's PSA began to rise again. How can one describe the raw disappointment, the fear we felt? Talk of radiation was another unknown to us. Stories of people who suffered aftermaths from radiation scared us. Again we were looking into a dark corner with no idea how to escape. Could radiation be trusted or would it create other serious problems? And yet….?

When I learned it is customary for radiation to follow cancer surgery, I became angry. It had not been done for Will. I was taunted for months, years. Perhaps I would still have my husband, *if* that treatment were given. Why was this not done? It was not even suggested by our Urologist. Why?

Thoughts of this conceivable negligence tore at me. I felt deceived. I felt Will and I were cheated out of life. Perhaps I used the doctor as a scapegoat, perhaps not. We'll never know. We understood there are no guarantee's in life. But my desperation to hold on to this man who fulfilled my life, wanted to lash out and strike anything, anyone remotely responsible.

We began making calls to well known Medical Clinics around the country. Being given a verbal picture of their treatment procedures, we finally made an appointment with Mayo Clinic in Rochester, Minnesota.

School was out for the summer and we were free to go. Jean and Don, our lifelong friends, came from Kansas to visit and helped us pack up for our trip to Minnesota. Not only was this a 'medical mission,' we used it to play out dreams of traveling through Utah and Colorado, visiting state parks, camping and loving our time together. We visited family in Kansas and traveled on to Waukegan, Illinois.

There we looked for the little cottage where we first began our married life. It used to stand next to 'the big house' where the owners lived, with open fields all around it, but that was over 40 years earlier. What excitement we felt when we did find it tucked in among a large community of homes! We stopped and knocked on the door of the 'big house', quite sure after all these years, it had changed owners. It had, of course, but at hearing our story, the present owner took great pleasure in talking with us and took a picture of us standing, once again, in front of our little honeymoon cottage.

We drove around looking for other familiar spots, particularly the beach we had spent so much time at, and the nostalgic downtown area. We were disappointed in finding that 'progress' had changed the scenery. And why shouldn't it? 'Our beach' was now replaced by a big yacht harbor; The Globe department store where I had worked, no longer existed, and malls had replaced the downtown shopping area.

We traveled through beautiful green Wisconsin, keeping an eye open for familiar landmarks of places we had once seen. We made our way into Indiana to spend a few days with Lorna's family who now lived in Fort Wayne. From there we went on to Mayo Clinic in Rochester, Minnesota.

Will's condition was evaluated and an appointment was made to return for radiation treatments. On our return trip a few weeks later, we went all the way to the eastern seaboard, visiting historic sites such as Virginia's Colonial Williamsburg.

What a wonderful experience that was, falling back into history and seeing life in action, as it was lived in the 18th century. It was a 'day in history' as we walked down brick lain streets of the village. Streets bordered with beautiful Myrtle's in full bloom and dotted with colonial dressed towns people. We observed silversmiths cutting intricate designs into silver spoons. We watched as a cobbler made shoes, wheelwrights, a cooper making barrels, potters throwing clay on a wheel and much, much more. This one day gave us just a taste of life in colonial times.

When we returned to Rochester, Minnesota, we found an apartment that had courtesy shuttle service to and from the clinic. But, we found the apartment to be very dirty. After a few tries to convince them what clean is, I resolved to clean it myself, if they would change the sheets and bring more to cover the living room furniture.

This was the best we found and it became our little home for the next 10 weeks.

We actually grew quite attached to it's quaint tone. Will's treatments were scheduled first thing in the morning and we had the rest of the day for ourselves.

We found a church that welcomed us. We even went on a weekend camping trip with them.

We traveled everywhere we could within a days' drive, enjoying the sights and sounds along the great Mississippi and inland. We savored the delicious taste of fresh corn that was sold from trucks parked on street corners all around town. On weekends, there were yard sales every mile or so, along the country roads and between small towns that had other things to do or see.

Discovering the character of our new environment, the many historical places and making new friends gave reason to delight in our time together without focusing too much on the dreadful reason of being there.

Rochester is best known for it's Mayo Clinic, but we discovered another point of interest, less known, yet significant to the tourists. As many as 20,000 to 35,000 migratory geese make their winter residence on the shores of Silver Lake in the heart of Rochester between September and February. Around 1,000 to 2,000 reside there year around. Should you choose to take a leisurely stroll on the walk way around Silver Lake you would best wear some rubber overshoes, as this is 'geese territory' and they 'go' everywhere.. …if you get my drift. Also the geese expect you to come with a supply of bread crusts as they are very friendly. What fascinated me most was to find a massive underground mall beneath Mayo Clinic. In the gift shops you could find lovely framed art called "Poop Art." It was a clever person who cashed in on the endless supply of dried 'poop' to create a piece of wonder!

When radiation treatments began, it was estimated to take four to six weeks, however there were some days Will just didn't feel well. Treatments were held off for a week or so until he healed. On those days, we just stayed in the apartment and worked on projects that we brought from home or just watched TV. I loved listening to weather reporters with their 'Minna-sooota' accent. But the highlight of TV viewing was seeing Minnesota's colorful new governor, the former pro wrestler, Jesse Ventura, with his piercing eyes. His wit and wisdom entertained us frequently and was arguably the country's most laid-back state chief executive.

Even though we were there for medical treatment, we loved being away from the responsibilities of home. On the whole, Will felt good and we had such a great time. It would not be easy to drag me out of there when the treatments were over. I did not want to go back home. Going anywhere together was always a special treat. Once in the car, we had nothing but each other and the road ahead to focus on.

"Hey, what do you say, we just keep going?" He would often say to me. "We'll call the kids and tell them where we end up." The fantasies we dreamed up could get quite elaborate, but ultimately we were brought down to reality.

This adventure had overlapped into the fall season and Will had a substitute that filled his place at school. Since Will had almost never taken a day of sick leave in the years of teaching, he now had built up enough days that his salary never wavered. Furthermore, we were blessed with a good medical insurance, and Will had wisely taken out a Cancer Insurance Policy at the beginning of that year, so the only out of pocket expenses we had were food and living. The generous insurance covered even that.

After two months of treatments were finished, the idea of returning home, going back to our work and daily routine was very hard. We had grown so comfortable in our life here. I dug in my heels. I was sure it would take wild horses to move me out of there. We had enjoyed such freedom to do the things we wanted without meeting any deadlines. As we left our 'home' in Rochester, we decided to take the long way home. Up through northeast Minnesota, briefly rubbing shoulders with a few Swedes on our way across North Dakota and on to Washington to see Chris and Rebecca.

We had never seen the Oregon coast and the ocean had always held such an attraction for us, so Chris and Rebecca arranged a camping trip and together we walked the beaches, picked up shells took pictures and watched the seagulls as they screeched and swooped down to catch their prey. We visited light houses on the cliffs overlooking the ocean and a historical Lewis and Clark site. We ate the 'catch of the day' at little restaurants resting on pilings that jutted out over the water.

This had been a splendid ending to our extended time away from home and it was time to make our way home.

Our Amazing Support System

Our children were an amazing support system! Although most of them lived a far distance away, their frequent phone calls and love sustained us. From time to time, they came, breaking away from their work and busy lives whenever possible to honor and bless us. Their gifts of love and concern for their father was a constant comfort for both of us.

Rebecca, Chris's wife, had already gone through a few years dealing with illness herself. She had contracted Lyme's disease, which left her debilitated and in need of treatment for a few years. Doing things for people, is a passion of hers. She had given many hours of loving nursing care to a man who lived near them. One she barely knew, who was slowly dying of cancer. Now, she unselfishly came for two weeks from Washington to monitor Will's diet and give herbal treatments, she read to him and pampered him in general. A special bond developed between them, through her generous gift of love.

Another time, Chris, Mike and Lisa came to spend a week cleaning out the barn and working in the yard. Once a vital cabinet shop, the barn had nearly gone to dust and ruin. On a stormy day earlier that spring a microburst hit the west side where a lean-to was attached. The roof had been ripped off and the sides caved in. This added a great deal of work, sifting through that rubble to salvage miscellaneous pieces of scrap machinery parts. One could not predict what you might find.

Mike and Chris were laughing and making a lot of noise about something they had found, so Lisa and I went to see what was happening. Just as if they had made a fast backtrack into their teen years, Mike and Chris delighted in waving this flattened mat of smelly, mangy fur at us. The poor cat had obviously found shelter there during the winter months and met it's ruin. It was this kind of playful humor and jokes they played on each other that made the task enjoyable.

Lisa's three daughters, Shandra, Katie, and Audrey coaxed rides from their uncles on the hood of Grampa's tractor as they made trips to the burn pile in the orchard. Running, jumping, tagging each other and taking turns on an old tire swing filled their afternoons. It seemed they were always begging for drinks or a cookie. But, squeals of laughter to the teasing and scuffling play that their favorite uncles dished out were some of the favorite delights.

This was life on 'Grampa's farm'. These are the echo's of children from generations past and the generation present that create memories to be tucked away for all time.

Adults, once children themselves, recall a time in years past, when they too came here to visit and play in their own Grandpa's yard. History had come full circle now. Not so much had changed, just the faces. Even the teeter totter with it's weathered old board, straddling a rusty old barrel remained, leaving splinters in 'little hinnies', same as in the early days. The adults look on, now as they take a moment from their purpose and hard work to reflect. They pleasure in the awareness of their mission. The opportunity to bring favor to their father.

Grandfather watches, from his swing under the tree, fondly listening to the children's banter. Pride swells up inside and he chokes back a tear as he witnesses this happy crew that has come to pay honor to him.

Time Quietly Slips Away

The summer passed. Will was excited to go back to teaching his classes at school. Anything less was unthinkable. In spite of the continuing trips to the doctor for blood tests and radiation treatments, nothing or no one could persuade him otherwise.

I would pick Will up after his classes at school and drive him to Pocatello for daily treatments. Travel, cancer, radiation and the daily classes wore on Will, so while I drove, he settled down in the seat and caught a nap.

We soon found that the radiation was not cutting the cancer. More aggressive treatments were given. With bouts of fear and grief sprinkled in, we were loving our life together in spite of the constant threat to our future. We continued living one day at a time, laughing together, crying together, talking, dreaming, and planning the rest of our life, regardless of the final outcome. We clung to our faith and hope in God, discovering that by keeping our eye focused on the road ahead, helped us keep our hopes up.

Grabbing this insidious threat of cancer by the horns, Will firmly resolved to give it the fight of his lifetime. He was strong and optimistic, ready to assure anyone who showed concern or fear in his behalf, things would be ok. His determination to live life to its fullest, exemplified the amazing force within him…until the Chemo treatments.

For a two month period the ravaging effects of the treatment robbed what quality Will embraced. There were times he was so cold. Hot water bottles, and piles of blankets, or pressing my skin against his….almost nothing could warm him until the awful chill ran it's course. A deep depression gripped him. I would hold him in the times he wept, or I would read Psalms and sing to him through the long sleepless nights. Because of the medication, his mind struggled with comprehending sometimes the simplest things. Doom hovered over him as relentless despair tore at his spirit.

"No more. I cannot live like this. I *won't* live like this," he determined and refused any more Chemo.

Throughout the six year journey with cancer, Will kept his eye aimed straight ahead. He fiercely rejected the idea of retirement. We continued to dream of places to travel, scheming how to see the world together . We sent for brochures for taking a cruise around the world by working on board a ship. Will started growing his hair long so we might take a summer and work together at Sturbridge Village in Massachusetts, a reenactment park of the colonial era. We made plans to do work on our own place to make it more saleable. Always planning ahead, never giving up hope. All the while, the slim reality of these things ever happening lingered in a secret place in the back of our minds.

Hope is an extraordinary spiritual gift of grace we are given to see us over life's rough roads. Martin Luther King, Jr. said it well.

"If you lose hope.
Somehow you lose the vitality that keeps life moving.

You lose that courage to be.
That quality that helps you go on inspite of it.
And so today I still have a dream."

❧

We had reached our 47th year of marriage.

Counting our courtship years, our love for a lifetime had lasted a half century. We were three years shy of the coveted 50th Wedding Anniversary. We had always counted on reaching this goal and agreed to do something great, just the two of us. Our dreams had been challenged, but we would not allow them to be taken from us.

Will presented me with a precious note he had written, expressing his love and devotion for me. In it he disclosed yet another fantasy; saying *"So many years, so many ways, you have supported my far out schemes. Now hear my new one. We have always wanted to take a cruise. We will sell out, convert everything to cash and set off around the world...."* He wanted so much from life!

And with a few more added lines..."

Since this may be as close as we get to our Golden Anniversary, I wanted you to have some Gold. I had some samples flown in from Alaska, but they were all very inadequate, so I had to catch an eagle. I hope you will come to love him, as he might get you out of a jam someday!" "My love always, Will"

When I opened the little package, there was a lovely gold chain and a bright $50 solid gold coin that would increase in value as time went by.

He was always thinking of little ways to care for me, take me places.... traveling so many far out places in our dreams together. I loved that about him. Knowing he would give me the moon if he could.

❧

It was becoming clearer to us that time and disease were taking its toll on Will. I sensed our traveling days were coming to a close. We decided to take one more trip with our camper to Washington to visit Chris and Rebecca.

This time, Will and I visited the coast by ourselves, enjoying some of the attractions between pouring rain. For Will, this was a deeply emotional time as he felt a certain finality. He wrestled with emotions, too numerous to count. He was torn between wanting to go home and spending a bit more time with this son he so dearly loved.

A picture that will remain forever etched in my memory is one of him alone at sunset. He sat on a log overlooking the ocean as the waves came crashing into shore. Deep in contemplation. Sensing his sadness, I went over and sat down quietly beside him. As I slipped my arm in his, I could see the tears glistening in his eyes. I felt this sacred moment with him as he bid 'goodbye' to the beautiful ocean that he loved so much, envisioning his own 'crossing the sea'. But the possibility of never seeing this beloved son again was nearly more than he could bear.

The Bionic Man

In the midst of this cancer battle, Will had a intense need to carry out his destiny. He heard about a Monastery near Twin Falls, Idaho and spent a couple days of prayer and meditation in the serene atmosphere. He came away with the desire to minister to those in prison and joined a Chaplain's Corp. The weekly Bible classes with the prisoners fulfilled a particular purpose for him. *"I, too, have a death sentence against me."* He would say. *"Mine is cancer."* He would proceed to tell them that he had no fear of death and how he found strength in his faith.

These are notes of his instruction to the prison inmates:

"When (God) allows problems or sickness to come into our lives, He is testing our reaction. He could have made us without choices, but he wanted us to have a choice so He would know that we love Him because of who He is."

"It was about 27 years ago when someone taught us this prayer. "Thank you, Lord, for giving me this opportunity to trust You. The Lord is unlimited in His resources and power."

Sadly, he had to give this up, as it was too much for him do this and teach school.

๏

Because walking had become so difficult for Will, he got a "wheelie" walker. One that you could push or sit on when he got tired. This would make it easier for him when he taught his classes and we put it into use when we went shopping. Walking through stores, he would often sit on it while I *slowly* pushed him around.

Over the years, we had so often enjoyed outings with our special friends, Norv and Arlene. One day we went to Pocatello together to have lunch and go to the museum at Idaho State University. On this day, it was a bit of a walk from the car to the museum door, so Norv offered to give Will a ride. Barely had they started, when they both went over into a heap on the sidewalk! Norv on top of Will! Horrified, I ran to Will, expecting to pick him up in little broken pieces, but he came up laughing! The front wheels had caught on the crack in the sidewalk. This was too close a call and we resolved right there, Will would never ride on the "wheelie" again!

While the 'monster' was invading more and more of his body, and the painful limp was progressively becoming worse. Will was taking more and more pills to dull the pain. When he consulted our Orthopedic doctor and found that he qualified for a hip replacement, he nearly danced for joy. It was a step forward. It was progress and he embraced the possibilities.

Managing the surgery and recovery extremely well, he took pleasure to learn that he now had a titanium implant. He liked to rate himself in the category of the bionic man. The doctor gave him a photo of the titanium prostheses to show in case a security alarm was set off. He enjoyed showing the photo to his students when he returned to school.

During his recovery time, Jean and Don came again from Kansas to visit for a month. They parked their big RV right next to our house. Their kitchen window lined up with my kitchen window so we could talk together while we prepared breakfast. What fun we had having meals together. We took scenic trips within a day's driving distance. We visited the "City of Rocks" in southwest Idaho and attended a colorful festival on the Indian Reservation. We played games and popped corn or just sat in the porch swing and talked about old times.

Jean too, was recovering from her hip surgery, so we had two walking with canes. They kept us entertained with their hospital stories and comparing their scars.

One comes to mind that gave us a good laugh;

A few hours after surgery, Norv and Arlene came to Salt Lake City to visit Will in the hospital. He was drifting in and out of heavy sedation.

After our friends left, Will became angry and reprimanded me severely for embarrassing him. "I couldn't believe it. You were going to the bathroom right in front of them...without even closing the door!" he claimed.

I couldn't believe I'd heard him right! I told him I'd only stepped in to wash my hands.

"But I heard you!" he insisted. And nothing could convince him otherwise. Even when I told him it was the drugs talking!

Jean and Will sat in the shade while Don and I picked ripe cherries off of our tree. Together we all pitted the cherries while we told story after story and laughed until our sides ached. Then Jean and I put together delicious pies that we enjoyed later. The month flew by so quickly. Summer came to a close and sadly it was time for them to leave for home.

About this time, Lorna, Brett and the children moved back from Indiana. Brett had secured a teaching position in the theater department at Idaho State University in Pocatello. It had been their goal to relocate back here to be near family and we couldn't have been more delighted to have all our children within reach again.

By then, Will was recovered. Much to his pleasure he was released by the doctor to start the fall term at school as well as drive the school bus again. The Bionic Man was back in action!

A Phenomenal Dream and The Sword

In the winter of 2002, scans showed Wills bones to be riddled with holes. The cancerous 'worm' had been eating away on him and there was no stopping it. Still we never gave up hope. There seems to be a fine line between being realistic and blindly hopeful at the same time, a positive defense mechanism, perhaps?

In early December we went to Montana to attend our granddaughter's ballet performance. Our first night there, Will raised up on one elbow in the night to adjust his position and I was awakened by a loud snap! Alarmed, we made assessment of what had just happened. We determined by the pain and weakness of his arm, that his collar bone had snapped. We placed his arm in a sling and added more pain medication. When we got back home two days later, the doctor confirmed our suspicions. Indeed, his collarbone had broken.

Not a whole lot can be done for that except to keep it immobile. It grieved him to realize this brought an end to his bus driving. He loved the kids. It was also a step backward. This also meant he could no longer get out of bed, so we got a recliner with a mechanical lift for him. That was his lounge as well as where he slept.

Although this also put a halt to our long distant travels, I still took Will to school each morning. Then I picked him up after class each day and took him to Pocatello for his treatment. We'd have lunch and head home for a long nap.

While we were in Montana, Will told Lisa of a scripture he had been reading and an interesting dream he had. Later he wrote about this experience.

"I had been reading the book of Isaiah when I came to the 38th chapter. Reading the story of King Hezekiah who had a very serious illness and the prophet Isaiah came to visit him. Isaiah said " God told me to tell you that you are going to die and to get your affairs in order."

King Hezekiah wept and cried out to the Lord. And the Lord said to Isaiah to "go tell Hezekiah, I have seen his tears, I have heard his prayers and I am going to give him 15 more years."

"I thought that was a cool story and I read it over and over. Several weeks later I had a dream in which I saw numbers rolling. I put out my hand to stop the numbers and they stopped at 7 24 2011. I immediately woke up and wrote them down. I thought it was an interesting dream and told several people about it."

"In Dec. when we were visiting my daughter and my collar bone was broken

Matt and Lisa gathered some friends and asked if they could pray for me. They invited me to come to their church the next morning and meet with their pastor who had survived a very serious illness that had taken him to the point of death. Lisa and Matt and their friends met there with us. and the pastor and his elders prayed for me. Lisa suggested I tell them about my 'numbers dream'. The pastor felt it was a very significant dream, and if the Lord confirmed that date I should proclaim it and he prayed about that too."

Then Lisa said "Daddy, I just saw a 'picture' in my mind of you, with a double edged sword in your hand. The date 7.24.2011 was engraved on it and you were thrusting it into Cancer. The sword representing the spoken and written word of God. The Lord is bringing a word to you."

"Since I have such a great interest in weapons, it took me only a few minutes to decide to get one, so Joan got me a double edged sword (made in Pakistan) for Christmas and we took it to a shop to have it engraved. It hangs on the wall by the table.

On the next Sunday, Will took the sword to church and told this story to everyone. Then taking the sword from Will and holding it heavenward, Pastor Race dedicate it as well as the date engraved on it to God's purpose.

With that, Will wrote finally, *"We are hoping and believing in God's confirmation, step by step, knowing there is no hope but thru God. Praise his Name."*

⤙

When Will went to have the numbers engraved on the sword, he told the man who would do the engraving the story of what the date represents. The man seemed very interested, and later we went back to pick it up and were about to leave, he said to Will. "See you on 7.24.2011".

The date remains a mystery that only God can reveal. Until then….. we wait.

A Special Family Christmas

Christmas 2002 was upon us with the usual bustle of planning and preparation . The tree twinkled with lights and bright decorations, with piles of presents covering the floor. The candles glowed a soft welcome as the temperature in the room rose and sounds became louder while the house filled with joyous noise of family coming together.

Still, there was a sense of foreboding that stirred in the shadows around us. It was plain to see Will's health was deteriorating. For this reason, everyone was present. Even, Norv and Arlene, our very close friends came to celebrate with us. Heather too, had brought a friend with her.

One more Christmas holiday! One more special time together as a family. There was an urgency to create new memories and reminisce of years long past. The house was full of people of all sizes. They were 'ours'. No one missing. Everyone was eager to make this a memorable Christmas as they had all been in the past.

We posed for family pictures while our friend Norv took them. These were precious moments to savor, preserving them for posterity and loving our time together, Most of all, honoring Will in the presence of his children.

We stretched the table as far as we could, improvising an extension and a card table on one end. I was determined to have everyone at the same table. The table and chairs filled the room from corner to corner. It was set with my finest white china, crystal goblets and bright red linen napkins to match the occasion. Delicious food crowded the table and every chair filled with happy faces, everyone holding hands as Will, the head of our family, said grace. Thanking God that each of our beloved children were present and for each life. Asking blessing on the food and our time together.

Dinner at the Harder's was a jolly scene, with everyone eager to tell their side of a story. It was suggested we go around the table, everyone telling about their favorite Christmas. Yet, tucked away in a silent corner of everyone's mind was the possibility there may never again be another celebration *just* like this one. These were truly cherished moments.

It always delighted Will to show his love and care in special ways. It was clearly evident in the extra spark in his eye about his gift for me. On our last Christmas eve together, he chose a special time when we were alone to present it.

He was beaming with excitement. As I felt the size and weight of this package that he eagerly handed me. I could see the sparkle in his eyes and the broad boyish grin on his face and an alert surfaced in my mind. I highly suspected *what* this gift was, and I inwardly prepared to meet his enthusiasm.

"Lord, help me accept this graciously. Help me not to disappoint Will," I silently prayed. I carefully opened it and it was, indeed, what I'd suspected. For only a second, I felt a stab of disappointment, but in that moment, God and I had a quick exchange. He helped me see Wills heart and I understood. I took pleasure in knowing Will's reason for giving this gift to me, thus, I could lovingly accept his offering.

For sometime, Will had spoken of my need for a Lady Weston handgun. One that was especially light weight and designed for women. Although I gently tried to dissuade him, it was imperative to him that I should have one.

I know Will was deeply mindful of my well-being. Equipping me with the knowledge and ability to care for myself, in his absence, was priority on his mind.

Will's long history of teaching his family self-defense and his concern for our safety was clearly represented here.

I will always treasure this gift. It is more than a weapon, it's a symbol of his love. It is one more measure of his care for me after he would no longer be around.

Never Quit Before the Finish Line

As Will's illness progressed, he grew weaker. The pain became more intense. This passion we had about touching became a life line. We leaned on each other. We depended upon each other physically, spiritually, and emotionally. I believe the real glue of our marriage, the bond that never broke, was our friendship. We began as friends and remained best friends forever.

Where ever we would be, people would delight in Will's pleasant demeanor that commanded their respect. A man who clearly dealt with serious health issues, who could embrace life with such optimism was to be admired. This was the case at our favorite restaurant. Nearly everyday, during the last months Will was taking radiation treatment, we went to Red Lobster for lunch. By this time, Will's appetite had decline, so we ordered the kind of food his stomach would tolerate and shared it.

We became well acquainted with the wait staff. Whoever served us always took a minute to chat and share a bit about themselves. One in particular, Terry would take a moment whether she was our server or not to scoot into the seat beside Will to, sit and chat for a minute. That became a regular thing when she was on duty. Sometimes she would sneak an extra 'goodie' for him. She was a lovely lady who knew how to brighten our day by showing that measure of love.

⚬

By now, he was on a heavy regiment of pain medication. He began to fall asleep easily anytime he sat quietly. In the middle of a sentence, while he ate, while someone was talking to him. I tried reading to him or watching movies together, but he would very soon fall asleep and no amount of stirring him awake would last for more than a couple of minutes.

Each evening after we finished our dinner, we reached for the game of Scrabble . This was one of his favorite times. While I put a round of 50's music into the player, he laid out the game. Invariably he would fall asleep, so I would say to him, "Will, it's your turn, honey" and he would attempt choosing his letters, but would nod off in the middle. So I would ask him if he wanted me to help. "Sure" he said, but often before I could make his play, his head would drop. He was off to sleep again. This went on for an hour or so, mostly I played both sides with him interacting in between.

When the board was full and all the letters were used, he would gather it up and say to me, "Thank you, so much for playing this game with me. It really means a lot."

We never kept score, we just played for the pleasure of doing something together. We, each had already won the prize.

⚬

In the mornings, after a bite of breakfast, he showered and I helped him dress, then off to school we would go. Just a few more weeks and classes would be over, but there was no stopping Will from seeing that he'd fulfilled his commitment to his students. He would see this through.

In fact at the end of school when contracts were handed out, Will signed on for the following year and began making plans how he could get an electric scooter to get around. At the present, he used his 4 wheeled walker and if he could, he would sit on it beside a student and help with a project.

Will's faith in God was unshakeable and exemplary of his life. This carried over into his classroom as well as to the colleagues he worked with. They saw his cheerful determination, his compassion for his students and they did what they could to lighten his load.

The superintendent told me sometime earlier, if there was anything at all that Will needed, I should let him know. Being the independent person, he was, Will was determined to help his students finish their projects in the last week of school; insistent on staying longer hours to get the job done. I knew he was too ill to do this. I felt this was the time to speak privately to his superintendent and ask for help. He thanked me and assured me not to worry.

That very afternoon, 3 men from the community showed up in the classroom and by the end of the week, the projects were done and the students pleased with their accomplishments. Will was overwhelmed at the generosity of these men. I later, confessed that I'd been tattling to the 'teacher' about him.

❧

April 10th Our 48th Anniversary! I wondered if Will had anything planned. When I picked him up at school, he instructed me to stop by the "Purple Pansy ". This was our local floral shop where he had ordered a lovely corsage for me. In the past he'd given me flowers, but this corsage

Joan Saner Harder

was a first! I was thrilled when he asked me out for lunch in Pocatello, too.

Will secretly planned to take me to a jewelry store. (Since I did all the driving, when I say "he took me" I mean he made the plan, and told me where to take *him*) It's an understanding that we had.

It was obvious the young man attending the store was curious as he watched an older gentleman leading his lady through the doors. Will, was in great need of support as he leaned heavily on his walker. Yet, despite his feeble appearance he upheld his stature valiantly, as he lead his beloved toward the counter.

The young man, noticing the corsage, sensed this was a very special occasion. He held back for a few minutes, giving the couple some time. Observing, while the two of them gazed through the glass counter at the lovely, sparkling pieces of jewelry. They were speaking quietly as they lovingly leaned on one another.

Then the attendant made his move toward them.

"Is there anything that I can show you" he asked cheerfully

I pointed to a pair of gold earrings that I liked and he pulled them out of the case.

Fingering them gently, observing their weight and design, then trying them on, I looked at Will. He asked if this is what I wanted. Looking into the mirror one more time, I looked back into his eyes, "Yes. But…, are you sure?" I asked, noticing the expensive price tag. Will simply told the young clerk that we would take them.

I was delighted and gave Will my warmest smile and 'thank you' hug. Keeping his eye on us, the young man asked. "How long have you been married?"

Of course, we proudly told him it was 48 years. Then he told us he was getting married in a few days and asked, "What is your secret to staying in love for that long?"

"Very simple, really," we told him. "Make sure you are marrying your best friend, and remember to say "I love you" many times daily. Communicate, listen, respect each other, trust and believe in each other. Play together. Don't keep secrets from one another and when times get tough never give up. And always be ready to forgive." "These are some of the lessons we learned."

He thanked us warmly as we turned to leave, saying, "I will remember what you said."

Will 'n Joan

Will greatly valued his independence. As his illness progressed, things became more and more difficult. Driving had been particularly hard for him to give up. He had never been comfortable in the car unless he was behind the wheel, but now he had to rely on me. I made it my mission to learn where the bumps in the streets were and avoided them or slowed to ease over them, as the slightest jolts could cause him to cry out in pain. I was now the one that came around to *his* side to help him out of the car, bring his walker to him and make sure he got out safely. Some of this was hard for Will as he always took such pride in being not only independent, but also the one to be *my* escort. Then I would remind him that we were a team and we pull together.

Some things became such a struggle, but we clung to each other for dear life. Every evening we sat together in each others arms, just soaking in the warmth of each other.

Sometimes he talked about his final wishes and I'd take note. He instructed me how to be safe, preparing me as best he could for my life to go on without him and to live it to it's fullest This was the most heart breaking part to listen to. He reminded me of his undying love and comforted me in my sadness.

Talking about these difficult subjects made everything seem so final. Yet they were so important, too. It was all part of the process.

I wanted to reject the entire prospect. "I don't want to accept this. How? How can I possibly live without his love?", my heart cried.

I didn't understand it then. I learned later, I would *never* be without his love. It is with me always. It's his physical presence that I would miss.

Repeatedly the enemy had drawn it's brutal sword and tried to rob our hearts, but nothing, no one could destroy that which we held so precious. We treasured our intimate moments together. Being in each others arms was a balm to our soul, whether it was a time of healing wounds or the simple joy of comfort.

Due to his inability to pull himself out of bed, he spent his nights in his recliner-lift chair, so sitting with Will on our sectional sofa, we could hold each other as we talked or watched a movie together.

Just as in our courtship days, nearly 50 years earlier, we could never be near each other without touching, caressing, and searching each other's eyes. There was something in that touch that soothed our spirits and held the promise of infinite love. We could never let go of each other for long.

When each blow became stronger and tried to threaten our resilience, we were reminded that over the years, through one struggle after another, we told each other, *'what matters most is that we have each other. What ever else may come, we will make the best of it'*. This is what we did.

The ground work had been laid years before, along with our commitment to each other and we knew our love could withstand any challenge. First and foremost, we were best friends.

Admittedly, it was a lot of added work for my body to handle, but I must say, doing things for Will, seeing to his needs gave me the greatest joy and pleasure. He made it so easy and I count it a gift from God to have this opportunity to serve such a man as Will. He was not one to give up. He made every effort to do what he could for himself, but more than anything, he never failed to lovingly acknowledge the little things I did for him.

"Thank you. You're so good to me" were the words on his lips, many times a day.

With that kind of praise and gratitude, I could not resist giving my all and looking for more and more ways to make him comfortable. When his legs began to swell and ulcers would break out, I did what I'd observed the therapist do. I gently massaged them with special cream every night. Gave him foot soaks and pedicures that made his feet look like he spent all his time in a salon. Touching him, loving him in this way was a sensuous intimacy that fed our souls.

I often sat and feasted my eyes on him, watching him as he chewed his food, drank his water, or as he talked, memorizing his every move, look and gesture. "Memorize, Memorize, Memorize" I would say to myself. "Never forget." I stored in my heart every feature of this man. Mannerisms too significant for me to forget.

I think I admired my husband more in his illness than anytime before. Certainly because life had became more precious, but for the courageous way he handled his illness, it made me cherish him even more.

Sense of Finality

Will did his grieving mostly in the night hours, alone, away in his own private sanctuary where no one could see. But I knew. I longed to be with him, hold him, to give solace to his grief, but I understood that he needed this time to pray and prepare.

These were the times he grieved for his family, prayed for them, treasured them.

These were the times he drew close to God for further instruction and ask for strength to finish his job here on earth with grace.

❧

We had attended a little church in Pocatello for some months now. We loved the people at "Christ Love Vineyard." and they highly respected Will. Our pastor asked Will to speak for the Father's Day service. He was not accustomed to speaking before a crowd and was reluctant to accept. He had grown much weaker and it was difficult for him to keep his thought patterns focused.

Lisa paid visits from Bozeman, Montana, whenever she could get away. It seems that each time they were together, a bond became richer between them. It was one of those weekends and she offered to help him.

They spoke together, taking turns talking about fatherhood from their unique perspectives. They spent a full day preparing together, working out who would say what.

On that Father's day, he sat before the audience in a chair with Lisa beside him.

The words that followed come from the transcript of their joint speech. They are a beautiful representation of the man whose life touched so many and who so many looked up to.

Ephesians 6:1 says: Children, obey your parents in the Lord; for this is right. "Honor your father and mother that thy days may be long in the land that the Lord thy God has given thee. "

"God wants to bless us, He wants to lavish His loving kindness on us. He gives us an awesome promise to do so and the command that will open us up to that promise: Honor your father and mother. God is sovereign but He is not pushy. He always gives us the option to chose our own way."

"I was 15. It was 1948 and WW2 had been over for 3 years, when one of my fathers best friends was murdered. Max was a sheepherder who lived in the desert, about 12 miles from town. He had been driving an old beat up '34 Chevy pickup and had just bought a brand new Dodge truck, but didn't get to use it very long before he was killed."

"The man who killed Max was a drifter. He took the rifle out of Max's pickup and shot him and buried his body under a heap of rocks. He took the new pickup , hauled all the sheep to market, then spent the fall harvest hauling potatoes and sugar beets for the local farmers."

"This was my dilemma in 1952. A man's life being snuffed out like this seemed so useless to me. Like the Good Samaritan we need to help our neighbor in trouble. I've always felt strongly that we need to be able to defend ourselves as well as others and our nation."

"My father, came from a long line of pacifists, and to him this was one of the most important beliefs of Christianity. When the Korean War started he was very much against my going into the military service and refused to let me take part. He said, that if I couldn't understand it now, some day I would."

"He did however think police work was ok. I was 62 when I certified as a level 1 police officer. While I will never compare what I did as a police officer with those who fought in Korea, I was very pleased that I could serve my community, my state, and my country in this way. I honored my father and was later able to fulfill my desires and experience the blessing of a deep inner satisfaction of knowing I had done my part.

God is a Redeemer. Because I did not go to war I worked at a VA hospital and ended up saving a man's life there."

"My father wasn't very personal. I didn't know him very well. So God didn't seem very personal either. He wasn't much of a listener. Perhaps more of an authoritarian. He did buy me a very nice shot gun, but almost never went hunting with me"

"Between the age of 21-42 I considered myself an agnostic. The only times I went to church was for my children's programs. I figured, if there was a God, he didn't have much to do with me, so I wouldn't have much to do with him."

"Fathers impart identity and a God concept. Somehow, even though I didn't experience that from my father, and even though I didn't have a personal relationship with God, God began the turning in my heart. I began to see the need to connect with my kids. I would like to stress the importance of fathers to build relationships with their children."

"There are many facets to being a father. Communication, listening, playing. We bought a canoe, something I'd always wanted and took the family canoeing in North California lakes, and San Francisco bay. Mike got interested in mini bikes, then graduated to a Honda 90 and Yamaha 125 which we all enjoyed. 4 kids - each with different needs/ personalities/ and interests.

Lisa added a few of her own thoughts:

"We went to movies together, or out to dinner or for ice cream. We went to the beach and once a year to the mountains to play in the snow. Dad took each of the kids with him to work and then for a treat. We also had individual campouts."

"Another thing that is truly remarkable to me is that Dad's family never said I love you. Yet Daddy always worked very hard to communicate love to us kids. I never ever doubted his love and that is the greatest legacy of all!"

Will continued to say:

"Joan faithfully took the kids to Sunday School and church. When Mike, our oldest son, was 12, he came to me and said he didn't want to go to church anymore. The kids at church were using pills and doing a lot of other stuff. I said 'OK. You can come work with me on Sundays' and I paid him $1 an hour, plus plenty of pop and donuts.

I believe that was one of the best things I could have done at that time. From there, our relationship grew and is very strong to this day."

"When Mike was 9 we went on our first back packing trip, following with many others. One summer we spent several weeks planning for a family trip into the Yosemite mountains. Mike and I built a pack frame for each one in the family. Joan, our 2 boys and 2 girls. Joan sewed the pack for Mike, and a sleeping bag for Chris who was 3 at the time. This was a memorable time for everyone. "

"One of my greatest sorrows, I remember from those days........at 10,000 ft going to sleep under the stars, Mike asked what I thought about all that stuff Grandma was always preaching about? I told him I really didn't know, but if I ever figured it out, I would tell him."

Lisa added:

"When we begin to turn our hearts toward God, He empowers us to begin to turn our hearts toward the other and in doing so, begins opening a way for them to turn to God also. I began turning to God and participated in the youth group at church. We began praying for my dad."

Will continued:

"Lorna and Lisa were very active in the church youth group. Through them and the pastor, God began to work. Pastor began having breakfast with me every week....

Listened to my way-out ideas."

"Mike took his motorcycle to Tahoe one weekend....and had borrowed my leather jacket. It rained and he loaned it to a guy and never saw it again. He came home quite upset, expecting me to be upset with him, but I said, something about if some one asks for your coat....give him your cloak also. It sorta blew his mind."

Ephesians 6:4 says: And fathers, do not provoke your children to wrath; but bring them up in the nurture and admonition of the Lord.

Lisa added,

"Mike began to see something of God the Father through Daddy. Because Daddy had turned his heart to God, his heart was opened up to Mike in a new way."

Luke 1:17 And he will go on before the Lord, ..., to turn the hearts of the fathers to their children and the disobedient to the wisdom of the righteous—to make a people prepared for the Lord

295

"*So often we make judgments about our parents. A judgment is a decision about the way things are. It's a way we have of distancing ourselves from the pain of disappointment. But if I put up an invisible barrier to distance myself from someone, that same barrier creates distance between me and everyone else, even God! We do it without ever putting it into words.*" We think. "*That's just the way fathers are and if God is a father, I'd better keep my distance.*"

Then Will closed,

"*That's what I did and I didn't even know it.*"

"*Many of you may have been deeply wounded, hurt, rejected, abandoned, abused. There are few who have never felt overlooked by their fathers or felt less important than the job or the newspaper or the TV. What has your response been? Have you dishonored your parents by tuning them out, by distancing yourself from the disappointment as I did?*"

"*I want you to know, God can make up for lost time. He can heal your heart and transform your relationships over time. Maybe its too much to turn your heart to your child or your parent right now. But if you will turn your heart to Him, He will begin the miracle process of transformation. Even if your parent is dead, even if you never even knew who they were, you can receive grace from the One who is the Father to the fatherless. He will meet you in your place of need. He'll wash away the hurt. He'll come and play with you and fill you with His unspeakable joy. Because it never is too late to have a happy childhood.*"

The Last Summer

The school year was now behind Will. I helped him put his class room and office in order. Some of his largest equipment was sold to school districts through out the state, leaving the smaller equipment in the expectancy of returning next fall.

At times it seemed his strength would increase, and we would be encouraged, but, only for a very short time before he would weaken again. It became more evident that this insidious enemy was rapidly charging forward to drive that final stake through his heart. When the pain level increased, he began to carry a morphine pump and took a regiment of narcotics, enough to hook someone for life.

He continued to loose weight, food no longer wanted to stay down, and he spent more time in his chair. All these signs indicated that he was failing. Still, he remained hopeful and 'failing' was *not* a word in his vocabulary. He would *not* give up. After all, in God there is always hope. But quietly, in his private time, he faced the fact that his life was being cut short and he continually made preparation for this event.

⭗

As the summer days grew warmer, Will and I would catch moments outside on the swing when the flies and mosquitoes were less aggressive. In those intervals we occasionally ate breakfast on the patio, sometimes lunch, as we spoke about a forgotten memory or sat quietly just being together.

During these times, Will would look over his 'kingdom' and still have visions of improving the landscape or some other project that could use a finishing touch. Such as getting the tractor painted. This little tractor was his pride and joy and it had become rusty over the many years. He felt it would not be saleable as it was. (He need not have worried, for later someone paid $2,000 for it.)

It frustrated me to hear him talk like this. To me, these were trivial things, but for him it was one of the goals he had set for himself years ago.

When he was well, his time was spent making a living. Now, in his illness, the desire to complete his goals still remained, but the strength was gone. He still tried to determine how the 90 year old rock barn could be stabilized.

For me, these things held no consequence. My primary goal was to do everything possible to keep my husband with me. Yet, perhaps in facing the final stretch of your life, unfinished things, regardless of their impracticality, loom large. His mind could not dismiss it, as mine could.

His goal was to make the things in his life as appealing as possible, so they could bring a worthy amount if sold. This was all a part of his master plan to leave me well taken care of.

Then the conversation began to drift to the ultimate phantom that emerged before us ....always there...always lurking in the shadows. I took notes as he talked about his final wishes, even as more dreams arose for 'tomorrow'. Neither one of us was ready to give up.

Last Big Hurrah!

On July 19, 2003, the gentle coolness of this rare perfect morning greeted Will as he went outside with his walker, to sit in his swing on the patio. He loved seeing the flowers at their best, the yard groomed and his favorite part was watching the hummingbirds as they fought for their territory over a feeder, just a few feet away.

Just as he took his place on the swing, Mike, Mary and Heather arrived. He was overjoyed. He felt honored to have them surprise him on this, his birthday.

For weeks, my mind kept turning to Will's approaching birthday. Over the years I've been curious to observe what seemed to me a pattern, that death often occurred very close to a birthday. I never knew if there was anything scientific to base this on, it is just my own observation. This idea kept haunting me, more and more now that Will's condition was worsening, and thinking this could possibly be his last birthday.

I decided to give him a party he could not forget! I created a list of our closest local friends, our children, of course, and our church family. Invitations were sent out, noting this was to be a surprise party for Will's 70th birthday. I planned the food, ordered a mountain of fried chicken and a decorated cake. Case by case, over the weeks, I brought in soda's and hid them, stocked up on ice, made baked beans and potato salad.

With the fruit salad and watermelon Lorna brought, there was enough to feed 30 people! What a feast and Will knew nothing!

I prayed for perfect weather in place of the strong wind that blew in off of the open fields and the desert beyond. I prayed for the absence of mosquitoes that swarmed in thick clouds, relentlessly landing in masses like miniature vampires to devour our blood. The combination of these obstacles plagued those of us who lived on the farm and would certainly ruin the party. Very little could be done about it. Still I made my plans and prayed.

We all marveled at the incredibly beautiful day that greeted us, like it was made to order; it was just the right temperature with little or no breeze. The obstacles that tormented us just days before were now gone and best of all *no mosquitoes !* There were no bugs of any kind for the rest of that day!

When friends began to arrive, car after car, Will's eyes grew large, wondering what in the world was happening. He had suspected nothing! Tears filled his eyes to see the yard fill with people we loved Each one coming to wish him a 'happy birthday' and give him a hug. Some would sit on the swing with him, or drew up chairs to be by him. Every one wanted to be near him. He was overwhelmed with the love and multitude of cards he was receiving. Each guest received a blessing from Will in return.

Nearly all who had been invited came. Even a few who just wanted to be a part of this special occasion. Eager to honor a man they all loved and respected. Intermittently, when I connected with Will, among all his admirers, he would express his amazement of how I could have pulled this off . What a thrill it was to see such pleasure reflected in his expression.

Everyone brought folding chairs and some extra folding tables. Soon the lawn was covered with people and the feast began. All the while our back door stayed open for constant traffic back and forth to the kitchen and bathroom. Guests remained until late afternoon and finally when the last one left. Will and I went inside, reminiscing over the details of the day. He kept asking me how I arranged all this without his knowing and spoke of it for days after.

Later, Pastor Race told us of a dream he'd had sometime earlier; there were cars lined up along side of the road and our yard was filling with people who had come to pay tribute to Will. That's just like God. He loves parties and He special ordered this day for Will, whom he loved so dearly and wanted to bless.

⌖

The evening, after Will's birthday party, everyone had left and we were ready to relax and talk about the day. Will was sitting at the table in his usual place and I stood behind him at the counter. Suddenly, he caught his breath and very slowly, with a monotone calmness, he said, "J-o-a-n, d-o-n-' t m-o-v-e."

I froze. I'd heard that same tone at times before and I recognized it as a warning.

Then again a bit less slowly, but with the same voice, he spoke again. "Look over at the basement stair way"…….. and there to my immediate horror was a small snake curled up on the carpet. First thing I noticed that I was barefoot and so was Will. Very slowly I moved around the far side of the table and made my way to the front door where our shoes were. Very slowly I put mine on and helped Will with his, while we formed a quick plan of action. He cautiously walked around the snake to the back door holding on to the counter and walls to steady himself. He found a pruning shear in the utility closet. My greatest fear was that the critter would panic and scurry down the stairs to the basement and who knows where we would ever find it....but it remained still. Will handed the shear to me. Mustering all of my nerve, I very slowly, lowered the shears over the snake and with one quick aim I caught it by the middle.... and with a sigh of relief and a shutter of gross panic, I carried this squirming viper out side and finished him off! Will was very proud of me taking charge like that! Me, so afraid of snakes! Well, lets say, I had a nightmare or two after that. Not one mosquito all day but the perfect day ended with a snake in the house!

I've often wondered why after the 30 years we'd lived there, this was the first time a snake found its way into our house. When we came from the city to the farm, that was my most dreaded prospect. I asked God to please *never* let me see a snake! Only once did I see a small garter snake near the house and only one or two elsewhere. And now..?

⚓

Before Mike and his family left that day, he invited his father to meet him the next weekend to watch the "Blue Angels" fly. This was a favorite event from the time Mike was a little boy, when we would go to the Navel Base in Mountain View, California. This was something our whole family enjoyed whenever they were in our vicinity.

Will was thrilled for the invitation and for one more thing he could do with his son.

Upon hearing of the event, our daughter Lisa and her daughters decided to came from Montana, to join us at the air show. Some of Mikes friends from Aberdeen came too and everyone eagerly helped in clearing the way for Will as he maneuvered his way through the thick crowd of people with a power chair we had picked up earlier that week. Through this crowd of people moving along very slowly, one step at a time, it took a great deal of concentration and energy for Will as he operated the hand controls on the chair, careful not to run into anyone. A very kind person who owned a hanger, observed Will's efforts and invited us to sit in the shade with them, a life saver as it was a very warm day.

Although, this tired Will out, and he easily dozed off from time to time, he rallied with a start as the planes roared past, never missing one. Will loved airplanes and had looked forward to this event. He cherished this opportunity to make more memories with his kids.

Defining Purpose

Your life is not defined by the last hit you take:
But by all that has built up to that point.
Which in the end, defines how you leave this life.
~Author Unknown~

The Oncologist and his staff had formed a great admiration for Will during those long weeks and months of radiation treatments. The doctor found it very difficult to tell us that particular day, that the cancer had now spread to the brain! Hearing this heartbreaking news, we clung to each other in silence, as we grieved……hopes were shattered in those spoken words. The doctor left the room to give us a few minutes to take in this new report.

The reality of this diagnosis took deeper root when his memory seemed to slack at times and his writing became difficult to read, food did not want to stay down and his head would sometimes drop as his sentences would trail off into slumber.

My heart cried a million tears, when I saw his pain and his gallant struggle without complaint, always gracious to receive help. I wanted to scream out in rage, yet I needed to remain strong. This was so hard. My greatest desire was to give Will the gift of dignity.

Throughout this journey we learned to process each 'wave' as it crashed around us. We grieved over it, talked about it, and finally conditioned ourselves to it, until the next wave hit. Then we would start over, almost finding a norm between each one, always silently questioning, 'Is this the last hit ?'

Will did not quit. No matter how hard life became or how disappointing, he refused to give up. I understand more now than I could at the time; why he would not retire so we could travel and play. Why he signed a contract for another year of teaching when clearly he was nearing the end? I know now that keeping routine in life was important in making it to the next day, the next week. The gentle disposition of this man, his love of good humor, the ease in his approach to things, and determination defined the purpose in his life. There was always a smile, a twinkle in his eye, a friendly hand shake, or a hug, no matter how tired or discouraged he became.

When all is silent with only the reflection of the past to accompany us, God has us in a place where we can recognize truth. He clearly shows us the original picture, then gently helps us see what He sees. If only we could teach our minds and hearts to listen to God's reasoning before jumping to our defenses, how much richer our lives would be. Yet, He is merciful to allow a second look at our foolish concepts and gently shows us the beauty and meaning of things we so wrongly perceived.

Together we learned, made mistakes and learned some more; sometimes holding on to each other with fierceness and tenderness, as we went down life's road, but always growing stronger with each mile.

❧

Will had many questions about Heaven. Sometimes feeling unworthy of God's mercies, yet joyful too of his destination. Our pastor Race Robinson spent time in prayer and council as he helped Will face the end of his life. Reassuring him of his destiny.

As time drew closer and it became certain that the end was near, I realized it was time to put some of Will's final wishes into motion.

It was a given that Ron Rodes, our old pastor and lifelong friend would tell Will's story from his perspective. I asked our current pastor to prepare something as well. Little did we know that one week later, they would be speaking before a crowd of people who had gathered to celebrate Will's life.

Ron, being Will's closest friend, spoke of the early years he'd known Will. A time when Will was grasping a fresh knowledge of Jesus Christ for his life. He also spoke of our close kinship. The many times they saw us through times of struggle, only to see us grow stronger.

Our pastor Race Robinson spoke of the past three years he had witnessed Will's battle with illness.

These are the words that reflect Pastor Race's thoughts as we celebrated Will's life:

"When Will and Joan first came to us at the Vineyard, it had been some time since Will had been diagnosed with cancer. I was immediately impressed with his unshakable faith every time he came forward for prayer. Will continued to believe, right up to the end, that God would heal him, as I did."

"As I was gathering my thoughts regarding what I was going to speak at his funeral, I began to dwell on the life of Will Harder as a teacher. Will taught woodworking at the high school. It was only fitting that his memorial service was to be held there in the school's auditorium."

"As I was meditating on this aspect of Will's life, the Lord began to show me how much a teacher Will had been to me. The incredible grace in which he lived the last few years of his life, and his unwavering faith, spoke volumes. Though the cancer and subsequent treatments were ravaging his body, I never once heard him complain. When he would see the sorrow and worry in my eyes, after hearing yet another negative report from the doctor, it would be him, encouraging me, not the other way around."

"I remember the last few days of his life at home on the farm. Bedridden with a morphine pump, which by this time, offered very little relief from the incredible pain, his only concern was the welfare of his children and his wife. There were many details to take care of, some small, some not so small, that had to be dealt with before he could go home to be with Jesus. I firmly believe that Will could have left this earth, and all the pain and suffering he was experiencing, long before he did, but his love and concern for the welfare of his wife, Joan, kept him with us until he was positive everything had been done to assure her financial security. I remember sitting at his bedside during those last few days.

Whenever the pain would be unbearable, Will would simply grip my hand and whisper, "Jesus," and the pain would seem to ease dramatically, as surprisingly, would the pain in my heart."

Reflecting back to the day of the funeral, Race told me:

"As I stood on the platform of the high school auditorium that day, looking out over Will's family, friends, students and co-workers, I shared with them how Will Harder was my teacher. Sent to me, by the Lord Himself, not only to teach me how to live, but how to die. I will never forget him and the priceless lessons he taught. I simply pray that I will have wisdom and the courage to carry them out.

"Fly With The Wind"

Go now, your faith has healed you You're free to dance
with me.
For it is by my Wounds that you are healed
And it is by my Cross that you are free
If you trust in Me than I will come. I will bring healing
on my Wings."
~By Katie Weaver

Katie was 13 when she wrote this song for her grandfather. When she came to visit from her home in Montana, just a few weeks earlier, she played the piano and sang it as a special presentation for him. With deep emotion, he listened intently, to the beautiful melody as she sang it in her sweet voice. The comfort he found in this loving gift, the words of this song gave peace to his soul.

The sincere, yet simple prayers of Katie and her sisters, Shandra and Audrey, spoken over their beloved Grampa, touched Will's heart deeply and gave him courage

᳭

We were preparing to go to Pocatello when hospice came to change his morphine pump. While we were talking Will suddenly grabbed his head and cried out with excruciating pain. Something that had not happened before. It didn't last long, but recurred a couple more times through that afternoon. By evening, he was too weak to move. The doctor ordered a hospital bed to be brought out the next day, but for now he was okay to stay in his recliner. I slept beside him on the sofa. Ready to do what ever he needed.

This sudden change hit us all with a terrible shock. We were already expecting the worst, yet we had no idea what it would look like. No matter how prepared, none of us were ready for this!

Our children made arrangements to come as quickly as possible. Mike arrived that evening. Our pastor and friends came from Pocatello to pray for him and helped in any way they could. Our friend, Donna, a registered nurse happened to have the week off. This wonderful lady stayed with Will, night and day, through out that week. Her husband, Buster went to his job during the day and drove the 50 miles out to spend the nights helping his wife care for Will. The only sleep they got were in short intervals on the living room hide-a-bed. Such love! I've never seen anything like this.

Others too, came out from Pocatello to offer 'day-care' for *me* at intervals; freeing me to spend my time with Will. Nearby friends and neighbors came to offer their support as they brought food and supplies. Our needs were well met. We were blessed!

Although Mike was very ill with a bronchial infection, he came the minute I called him and for that whole week, he gave his utmost support to me and care to his father. The rest of the children came one by one, from Portland, Montana and near by to have their time with their father. Heather too, stayed by his side, administering loving support to her grandfather. A difficult time. A precious time that will linger in our memories forever.

Only one person was missing. Mary, Mike's wife. She had gone to New York on business just the day before this last strike hit Will. She was due back home by Sunday, but as fate would have it, New York City experienced a total power outage and there was no transportation out. She was stuck indefinitely, painfully isolated. It was so difficult for her to be separated from her family at a time like this. Our family needed her. This added another blow to our sadness, particularly for Mike and Heather, who longed for her comfort. Will noticed her absence right away. He held a special love for Mary, and admired her very much. Now he was asking for her.

At first, when he was put into the hospital bed, Will insisted he could still get up and to use the bathroom. Assisted with one son on either side, Will very slowly pushed his wheeled walker to accomplish his mission, then returning him back to his bed. Such an ordeal took a long time, yet he was not ready to give up. This, however, only lasted a day or two.

The seizures occurred more and more frequently and with each one, we prayed for it to cease. Fortunately they didn't last long and when they were over, Will would always say, "Thank you, Jesus." He found it difficult to stay awake when people came to see him, but weak as he was, he never let one of them leave without a blessing and a gracious thank you.

Because I had so much help, I was privileged to sit with Will and give him drinks of water, just hold his hand, or help him when he needed to empty his bladder.

Everything had already been said, many times over the past months and years. We had long ago given and taken forgiveness over hurts that were far behind us. All we had left was to give reassurance of our untarnished love for each other that would span eternity. During one of those times, I asked him to 'marry me again'....'right now, this minute' and he smiled his approval.

His eyes had always given me so much pleasure. Such a soft blue. So gentle and expressive. As I looked deeply into his eyes, one day, I said to him,

"I love your beautiful blue eyes." After just a moment of thought, he said slowly and deliberately,

"My beautiful blue eyes are for you to enjoy."

The final stretch of road grew shorter, I observed him looking off into the distance within the close quarters of the room, as if gazing into a realm never seen before. Beyond this veil, into a dimension that only he was privileged to see....and I knew.... *I knew* he was being given a preview of the glory to come. He was ready.

⚘

Everyone had gone to bed and I was alone with Will. The fans were shut off now, for finally, the blazing heat of the day was replaced by a cool night air, gently blowing in through the window at the head of the bed. A few crickets could be heard chirping merrily outside. The only sound in the room was Will's breathing and occasional outcry of pain, yet even that had diminished some, thank God.

I sat on a high stool and lay my head on Will's pillow, humming softly to him, praying for him, whispering sweet things, releasing him to God. Telling him, "I love you.". A CD by Brian Doerkson was playing. The soft melody and words sounded as if they were straight from Gods heart, whispering...

*"Son, you are my treasure. Son, love beyond measure fills
my heart for you.*

*My son, I want to be your friend, to walk beside you
until all life shall end.
Every song you hear will whisper that my Love is near
Golden notes and melody touch your heart in harmony.
You are my son."*

Immersed in these precious moments throughout the night, I felt the quiet, peaceful presence of the Almighty God, spreading his Love over both Will and myself.

….Then came morning .

Lorna arrived before dawn. She and Mike sat by their father until the sun came up, allowing me to doze off on the sofa near by. Ready to wake me at a moments notice.

Someone had told me Will might be holding on for some unfinished business. I couldn't imagine what that could be, until it occurred to me he might still be concerned about his provision for me and I knew what I needed to do. How I hated to leave that morning. I tried to dismiss the idea from my mind….but if it would give him peace, I would do it.

I leaned close to his ear and told Will, "Darling, it's important that I run into town for a few minutes. I don't want to go, but I must. I love you with all my heart and I'll be right back." Caressing his cheek with my lips and a squeeze of his hand, I walked away.

Our dear friends of many years, Norv and Arlene were there holding vigil with us. Norv took me to the school where I met with Will's superiors. Possibly the biggest reason Will had signed a contract for this next term was to hold onto his retirement. He had worried for weeks earlier when he turned 70, that it might be lost if he didn't show up for the beginning of the new school year which was beginning in just one week. But the principle graciously assured me there were no worries. Will's retirement was safe.

I felt such an urgency to rush back home to tell him. As I left the building, the atmosphere seemed to have a strange, surreal haze about it. Almost as if a veil had been drawn over everything. When Norv came to pick me up, I was already beginning to panic. I wanted to scream for him to drive faster! He couldn't get me home fast enough.

When we drove into the yard, Mike and Arlene met us at the door......I knew!

I brushed past them to Will's side, in hopes there was still a breath of life left in him. But, he was so still. He slept so peacefully. Putting the side of the bed down , I crawled in beside him. I gathered Will in my arms as I'd wanted to do for so very long.

Cradling his head on my shoulder, I wrapped my arms around him and snuggled in. Nothing couldn't hurt him now. He felt no pain. So long, it had been since I could hold him and squeeze him like this!

So long, I had longed to pull him against me so tight! My heart cried out. I whispered, over and over, "I love you, I love you, my precious darling." His eyes were closed now. Never again, would I gaze into his beautiful blue eyes. Never again, would I feel his warm breath on me. I kissed his lips, his closed eyes, his head, his ears as I held him tight. This was my lover. He had been so sick, every touch so painful, yet now......

Suspended in time, I remained there. Holding him, loving him, resting as I enfolded him in my arms. I wanted to never let him go. His spirit was souring above and I believed he had to know what I was feeling just then. Even in the 'glory' of being with his Heavenly Father, he knew my grief and perhaps he felt the sadness too. I believe he knew the love of my arms around him.

❧

Prior to that final moment and many times throughout that week, Mike kept close vigil at the side of his father. And several times in the last hours, he would release him, with a promise…..

"It's ok, Daddy. You can go. We'll catch up with you"

And now…. in Will's final hour, while I had gone on a 'business mission' in his behalf, Mike and my dear friend Arlene sat by his side. Mike sensed a change in Will's breathing. Seeing his father gasping for his breath, Mike picked him up in his arms.

"Fly with the wind, Daddy" Mike said, "fly with the wind."

Will drew his last breath in the loving arms of his first born, as his spirit drifted heavenward.

"Fly with the wind, Daddy, fly with the wind. We'll catch up with you later."

Epilogue

*For I know the plans I have for you," declares the
LORD"......
"To prosper you, to give you hope and a future, to give
you an unexpected end"
Jeremiah 29:11 Paraphrased 'The Message'*

Is it possible for a random event that happens in childhood, to be a forerunner of things to come? A promise of tomorrows that only God can see, so far ahead in time, yet unimagined in our minds? Does God prepare a road map of things to come, only to be seen much later when we look back?

One of my early memories as a child of 5 is attending a church picnic with my parents at someone's home near Whitewater, Kansas.

I remember driving down a long lane before approaching the house, and I remember the large lovely meadow where lots of people were gathered in the shade of some trees.

At some point my mother and I were in the little garden area by the back door at the house. A few other children were playing there, but I felt ignored and alone. No one offered to play with me. No one knew me. So, I watched as the others played. My attention turned toward the sound of

317

water running in a near by corner and I was fascinated by what I saw.

There was a statue of a boy and girl leaning back to back under an umbrella, looking over their shoulders toward each other. It appears the boy has just given the little girl the bouquet of flowers she held in her hand. Her eyes were shyly looking down; both smiling. Rain was dripping down over the umbrella around them into a small pool. A fountain. Something beautiful. Something with no other purpose than to give pleasure to the observer. Never had I seen anything so lovely. The image stayed in my memory, to resurface years later when Will and I were sharing memories of our childhood.

For a very brief period after my family moved to El Dorado, my parents, attended the Mennonite Church in Whitewater Kansas, about 30 miles from our home. They drove the distance on gravel roads in an old car nearly every week for a time.

For Will's family and relatives this was their home church. It so happened that his family was preparing to move to Idaho very soon. He too, had similar memories; the long lane, the house, children, the fountain. Perhaps this was the last event they attended before their move. Could it be? Was it possible that Wilfred was a shy little boy who stood somewhere near me that day? Could this be an indication of the amazing ways God orchestrates our lives from beginning to end?

After our discovery of similar memories, my heart could not let go of the picture of the fountain. I felt I must have one as a reminder of a dreamlike, yet probable occasion we may have shared together, years before we would actually meet. Drawn by an invisible tie that bound us?

A young man from Idaho and a young woman from Kansas would come together. Unaware of the destiny in life that was designed for us long before we fell in love and married.

The first summer after Will's death, I took a long road trip to rediscover myself. In a garden shop along the way, I found a treasure. In a corner of the shop, half-hidden among old discarded statues, stood a little figure. It was the same little boy and girl that had stood under the fountain umbrella 60 years earlier and captured my imagination. She still held the freshly picked bouquet. She still looked down shyly. He still smiled. Adoring her. Forever.

I Know You By Heart
I see you.
Breathless.
My lungs cry out for air
When you touch me. I want more
I nearly faint with need
We're so young
So innocent
Your manliness makes my fever rise

Your hands. so strong , yet
There's a delicacy about them.

Your arms. smooth .soft. silky blond hair that glistens in
the sunlight
The way you smell after a shower or as you came in
from the cold
The fragrance of your after shave. mixed with the
flavor of Juicy Fruit
You arouse my senses.

Your wild laughter when I touch your tickle spot
The little nub on your leg
I love your toes because they are yours

The smoothness of your lips
The way you give them a quick lick before you speak
The wetness of your tongue when you kiss me
The tilt of your mouth
The heat in your eyes
These things I will never forget because
I love you. I remember you. I know you by heart

Gently you approach me

With passion in your eyes

Innocence gone. We have succumbed to our desire.
So gentle is your touch, so hot is your hand as you map
out my body
Our breath quickens as we know each others passion
So sweet, so tender
Our love together ascends to heights of ecstasy
Let us remain forever....in that realm

Our eyes meet across a room
Your wink. Oh, your wink. Be still my soul!

Your touch on the small of my back as you guide me
through a crowd
You reach for my hand, no matter where we are.
You are always there, assuring me, caring for me

I listen to your voice.
I hear you sing to me: 'O buttermilk sky.'
'Have I told you lately that I love you?'
Your voice stirs my heart I fall in love again and again.

I remember you, my darling
I fall in love, each day
Still
And when we meet again
I'll know you by heart.

~Written by Joan Harder 2005~

Acknowledgments

First and foremost, my eternal gratitude to Will Harder, the man of my dreams, the man who gave this story life and inspired me to spread my wings and fly.

To my daughter, Lisa Weaver, author of "Beautiful Destiny", who guided me through the past two years of this writing. My gratitude for the many long hours you spent lovingly editing and teaching me so many things about word structure and story writing. Your amazing gift with words has been an inspiration to me.

To my granddaughter, Shandra Weaver, Masters in Architecture. I admire your insightfulness, and perseverance. And I am proud to present a small sample of your talent on this lovely book cover you created for me.

My thanks to Gloy Wride, who inspired my daughters, by opening their world to writing in their high school years. When you critiqued the first draft of my manuscript, you set me on course. Your inspiration as a teacher and a friend served to bring this to completion.

Donna and Buster Smith, the compassion and love you showed Will and our family in his last days will never be forgotten. What an incredible gift!

To all of you; my children, family and friends, who have given of your strength and love in countless ways.

Those of you who have stood with me in the most difficult time of my life. You have taught me to live again with hope and joy. I am so grateful for each of you. The list is so long, but *you* know who you are. Thank you for believing in me. I love you.

-Joan-

9 781449 711658